"As a fledgling lawyer struggles for traction, practical wisdom about the nuts and bolts of success is vital, but often missing. Reading and heeding the good counsel in *Raising the Bar* will make a significant difference for the better."

W. Taylor Reveley III, *Former President, The College of William & Mary and former Dean of the Law School; Former Managing Partner, Hunton & Williams, USA*

"JB Burtch has devoted his distinguished 50-year career to modeling the heartful wisdom contained in this essential book . . . a must-read for any new lawyer.

Raising the Bar successfully brings to the printed page JB's master-level, hands-on mentorship, which helped this lawyer get his professional footing and launch a successful start-up."

Daniel Seaman, *Founder, Optimus, USA*

"*Raising the Bar* should be standard reading for new lawyers, no matter the setting in which they practice. Allowing lawyers to find their version of success is JB's gift – and now his wisdom and guidance are available to everyone launching a legal career."

Henry D. W. Burt, *Chief Administrative Officer, Troutman Pepper, USA*

RAISING THE BAR

RAISING THE BAR

THE MENTOR GUIDEBOOK FOR NEW LAWYERS

JACK W. BURTCH, JR.

informa law
from Routledge

Designed cover image: Lucie Kasparova/Getty Images

First published 2025
by Informa Law from Routledge
4 Park Square, Milton Park, Abingdon, Oxon OX14 4RN

and by Informa Law from Routledge
605 Third Avenue, New York, NY 10158

Informa Law from Routledge is an imprint of the Taylor & Francis Group, an informa business

British Library Cataloguing-in-Publication Data
A catalogue record for this book is available from the British Library

Library of Congress Cataloging-in-Publication Data
Names: Burtch, Jack W., Jr., author.
Title: Raising the bar : the mentor guidebook for new lawyers / Jack W. Burtch, Jr.
Description: Abingdon, Oxon [UK] ; New York, NY : Routledge, 2025. |
Includes bibliographical references and index.
Identifiers: LCCN 2024031131 (print) | LCCN 2024031132 (ebook) |
ISBN 9781032876375 (hardback) | ISBN 9781032876290 (paperback) |
ISBN 9781003533672 (ebook)
Subjects: LCSH: Law—Vocational guidance. | Lawyers—Professional relationships. |
Attorney and client.
Classification: LCC K120 .B85 2025 (print) | LCC K120 (ebook) |
DDC 340.023—dc23/eng/20240714
LC record available at https://lccn.loc.gov/2024031131
LC ebook record available at https://lccn.loc.gov/2024031132

ISBN: 978-1-032-87637-5 (hbk)
ISBN: 978-1-032-87629-0 (pbk)
ISBN: 978-1-003-53367-2 (ebk)

DOI: 10.4324/9781003533672

Typeset in Times New Roman
by Apex CoVantage, LLC

This book is dedicated to my students.

CONTENTS

Introduction

This is the book I did not know I needed when I began law practice. But now, having spent my career as a lawyer, I can write the book that will give new lawyers the edge they need to accelerate their practice to a higher plane. The first years out of law school are difficult. Most of what a lawyer needs to know about law practice is never taught in law school. We pick it up on the job.

This, of course, has always been the subject of debate. Should law school teach students how to practice law or how to think like a lawyer so they can learn to practice? This book avoids that debate. It accepts that, emerging from law school and passing the bar, new lawyers need to be exposed to practices and ideas that are rarely encountered in school but are necessary for professional competence. My goal here is to accelerate the process of becoming a lawyer able to practice law at a level of professional accomplishment.

I've been licensed since 1972. Most of my practice has focused on labor relations and employment law. My career has been centered in Richmond, Virginia. Over the years, I've practiced in a large law firm, a medium-sized firm, and several boutiques. For over 30 years, I've also been an adjunct professor of law and taught hundreds of law students. Many of them have kept in touch after leaving school, and I've been privileged to encourage them at turning points in their careers. While each personal situation is different, themes do emerge. How do I fix a mistake I just made? How long will it take until I know what I'm doing? Do I really want to be a partner in this firm? Most of us lawyers have confronted these questions. It is much better not to do it alone. This book is your companion.

It was November 1972. I was in the Army at Ft. Lee, Virginia, finishing my basic officer training when the Army told our class it had too many second lieutenants and was releasing all of us to the Reserves rather than sending us to Vietnam. Married, living in a trailer park outside Petersburg, Virginia, and about to be unemployed, I needed to find a job. Only one firm in Richmond would even give me an interview. I had grown up in Ohio, gone to a New England college and a Tennessee law school. At that time, this was not the background prominent Richmond, Virginia, law firms desired for their new

DOI: 10.4324/9781003533672-1

associates. But the firm that gave me a chance had an influx of employment work and its labor section needed more bodies to do that work.

On February 12, 1973, my wife drove me to the front of the firm's office building, and I began my legal career. The first day was mostly administrative. I was introduced to the lawyers in our section and then put in the care of the secretarial supervisor for firm orientation. The group was composed of five new secretaries and me. The supervisor explained that employees had to account for at least 7½ hours worked each day. Immediately after saying that, she turned to me and said, "But of course you'll be working a lot more." I was already nervous and uncomfortable. I was insecure about fitting in with the Virginia culture, and this was the second time that morning someone had intimated the firm's intention to work me to the limit. I did not want to fail at my first shot at being a real lawyer. I felt I had stepped into a different culture where the language seemed to be English, but the meaning was not easily apparent. I would not only have to learn how to be a lawyer, but I would be taught by people whose assumptions and traditions I did not yet understand.

The leader of our labor section was a Dartmouth graduate who served in the Navy during World War II, graduated from the University of Virginia Law School and was now the preeminent labor lawyer in Virginia. A gruff man who chain-smoked Camel cigarettes, he was said to have a heart of gold, but I questioned if I was ever going to see it.

I was wrong. I saw it that first day. As we were ending our initial conversation in his office, he abruptly changed the subject. "JB," he said, "I want to tell you something, and I want you to listen." He lit another Camel. "If anyone ever tells you to do something you believe is wrong," he exhaled a puff of smoke, "don't do it. Come see me." There it came, my first day on the job, when I was scared and feeling completely inadequate. I was reminded in crystal-clear terms of the highest standards of our profession. Not only was I expected to behave as an ethical member of the bar, but I had someone covering my back. In his direct way, our team head had reminded me that I was a lawyer, part of an honorable and ethical profession.

Each firm has its own personality and culture – some healthy, some toxic. What a firm is really like on the inside is hard to discern from the interview process. But once inside, there are distinct strategies to help the new lawyer chart a course to achieve personal success. While law firms may put sophisticated titles on what they do, firms primarily live and die by sales and production. With no capacity, there is nothing to sell. With no clients, there is nothing to produce.

There was a time when experienced lawyers passed on their knowledge of how to practice law to junior colleagues. While the mentoring tradition exemplified by the labor team's leader has not disappeared completely, true mentoring has become increasingly rare. Time pressure, economic pressure, and technological innovation have combined to make this learning experience less available to the new lawyer. Rather than bemoan the loss of this training, the challenge is to introduce the new lawyer to the craft of law practice in a way that is accessible today.

The old system that trained me was far from perfect. Not all experienced lawyers were reliable mentors. The new lawyer learned the craft by observing what other lawyers did well or, even more instructive, where they fell short. The rule of thumb was it took five years in practice to become a competent attorney. The process still takes time. It involves exposure to different kinds of clients and different kinds of challenges to transform a new lawyer into an experienced lawyer.

Becoming an effective practicing lawyer on your own, without significant mentoring, is an uphill slog. If you do not reach out to experienced lawyers for guidance, the road will be more difficult. Whether you begin practice in a small or a large firm, or even as a solo practitioner, seeking the guidance of more experienced lawyers pays continuing dividends. One benefit is less obvious than just getting a head start on how to approach a new challenge. Lawyers who seek mentors tend to become lawyers who are mentors. There are few better ways to stay up to date on the trends of the profession than to befriend younger lawyers. It's an investment that keeps paying interest.

Law is more than a career; it is a profession and a vocation. A profession connotes an occupation that is acquired only after a long period of education and training, leading up to some type of formal license or certification. A vocation suggests an occupation to which the individual feels a sense of internal motivation and dedication. Some individuals decide to become lawyers because they think it is a solid, well-compensated job for which they have the intellectual capacity and work ethic to succeed. And some of these lawyers have made successful careers in the law without ever feeling they were especially called or devoted to it. Others have left the law for entirely different pursuits or have entered jobs tangential to the profession. There are many ways to serve as a lawyer. Career satisfaction results from discovering the path that leads to the destination you desire.

Today, the practice of law is in the middle of a technological revolution. Whole areas of what used to be law practice are being taken over by computer programs and artificial intelligence. This presents both challenges and opportunities for new lawyers. The experience of new lawyers learning their craft is going to be different from the experience of lawyers in previous generations. Lawyers learn from experiences, but only so far as they inform principles. This book encourages the new lawyer to engage in deliberate reflection on the processes of law practice. Experience itself is not enough. To learn from experience, we must analyze it.

In this time of proliferating digital solutions to traditional problems, some see law practice as just one of many alternative vehicles delivering legal services. Some lawyers feel threatened by this. For the best lawyers, however, it is not a threat at all. Judgment and wisdom are not commodities. They are impossible to automate and scale. While much of the work we have been trained to do has become automated, how we apply that work and how we counsel clients based on their values and objectives will remain an art, not a commodity.

Lawyers solve problems. Their tools are the legal system, its precedents, procedures, and rules. But the point is to solve the problem. This book intends to guide the new lawyer in navigating the system to arrive closer to a real solution. Consider this book a jump-start for your legal career.

One place to begin the journey toward becoming an accomplished lawyer is to ask, "Why did I want to become a lawyer in the first place?" This is a question worth taking some time to ponder. Perhaps you felt the lawyer's role resonated with your own sense of identity. Maybe you enjoyed the process of figuring out problems or helping people in trouble. Perhaps you were energized by competition. Maybe you saw the law as a path to a more just society. Whatever your reason, tapping into that deep source of motivation while performing your everyday tasks will enhance your personal satisfaction and help avoid premature burnout.

Some years ago, I had a conversation with a friend of mine who was a bishop in the largest diocese of the Episcopal Church. Before going to seminary, he had dropped out of a prestigious law school after finishing his first year. He knew I had made a deliberate choice to go to law school instead of seminary and was interested in how I had managed to complete law school. I told him that being a lawyer gave me an internal sense of accomplishment and purpose. He told me that after his first year of law school, he could not imagine spending his whole career in "the tedium of the law." Having read volumes of mind-numbing federal regulations, I am quite familiar with the tedium of the law. But what gives me great satisfaction is that, knowing the law, I can make something happen, prevent it from happening, speed it up or slow it down, all depending on what the client needs.

A legal education provides knowledge and skills that are not tested on any bar exam. But these are key to the lawyer's functioning role within any community. The tedious process of reading hundreds of appellate cases, briefing them using the IRAC (Issue, Rule, Analysis, Conclusion) method and being ready to defend positions through Socratic dialogue produces minds that are comfortable with making fine distinctions and isolating separate issues, even under pressure. Thus, when considering any fact scenario, the lawyer instinctively seeks to separate the key issues from the ancillary ones. Legal analysis, which breaks down problems into component parts, identifies the decisions that need to be made. Reformulating the client's concerns into discrete issues and essential decisions clears the path to the client's desired result.

Incremental change can give me a sense of accomplishment. Even when my cause fails, I have done something to shape a situation, so my client's position can be improved. For me, enduring law school and the bar exam opened the door to helping people and organizations solve their most important problems. While the glow of psychic satisfaction has not shown up every day, it appears more often than enough to confirm my original choice.

Law firms are service organizations. They produce very little for themselves. Their efforts are directed toward helping clients solve problems and representing clients in legal processes. It is important for the new lawyer to grasp this fundamental reality. Very few lawyers work for their own purposes. Even lawyers who serve advocacy groups aligned with their own ideals are subject to instructions with which they may not agree. For many lawyers, working for an advocacy group is one of the great attractions of the law. By helping other people and institutions achieve their goals, we can participate in building a more just society, one matter at a time. The adversarial system within which we operate values fairness and acts as a constant counterbalance to oppression. Plainly, there are influences of wealth, power, and privilege that must be acknowledged and limited. The adversarial system has removed many systemic injustices of the past as it continues to be refined. But people who are not motivated to serve others are not likely to find the law to be a satisfying career.

Today, a law school degree and bar membership open the door to a profession almost unlimited in scope. Even at a time when the practice of law is challenged, there are certain foundational principles the successful lawyer needs to absorb. The quicker that happens, the greater the new lawyer's advantage. Law is a profession that, if we keep our wits and energy, we can practice into what others consider to be old age. It is a profession that offers to transform our experience into judgment and our judgment into wisdom. No matter what economic forces or technological changes may bring, wisdom will always be valued, and our skills will always be in demand.

Welcome to the practice of law.

CHAPTER I

Building Your Career

From about the age of ten, I wanted to be a lawyer. Growing up in a small Ohio town, I saw lawyers as those to whom people brought their problems, told their secrets, and relied upon for guidance. Once, as a child, I wanted to borrow a green leather box from my father to hold my important papers. (That I had "important papers" at age ten was a sure sign I was destined to be a lawyer.) One of our town's lawyers was visiting us that day and suggested I lease the box from Dad. "Lease" had a nice legal sound to it. He hand-wrote a brief contract that satisfied both father and son. We signed it and then he presented me with a bill for $1.00 for his legal services. (Of course, I didn't have to pay it, but I guess he wanted me to learn, early on, that fees are incident to the service.) Most people do not get the lawyer bug that young. Some wander into the profession in search of meaningful work; others figure out law is something they enjoy and can do well. But from that early age, I saw lawyers as problem-solvers and community leaders. That was a role I wanted to fill.

Our legal careers are shaped by choice, chance, and effort. Our choices determine our direction. Chance determines what opportunities may be available, but effort determines how we will use those opportunities. Going to law school and practicing law were choices. Using intelligence and grit to achieve good grades and pass the bar exam took effort. While the opportunities we seek may seem out of reach now, we are not helpless pawns in a mysterious game controlled by hidden powers. Opportunities are presented or created. The key is to identify opportunities when presented or to recognize challenges with solutions that become opportunities. The combination of our choices, our effort, and our opportunities defines the course of our legal career.

Today the whole concept of career is in a process of transformation. The former model of gaining skills for a line of work and progressing along that line died some time ago. Different models are emerging to suit different personalities and endeavors. Obviously, people want physicians with specific education, practical training, and experience. Lawyers need sufficient legal education to pass a bar exam. Beyond that, there are many different paths.

DOI: 10.4324/9781003533672-2

Here, career means the path you choose, assuming you are a law graduate, licensed or becoming licensed. Yours may be a path from associate to partner to retirement from the same firm. However, that is increasingly unlikely given the transformation of work life occasioned by the digital age and a clearer understanding of family needs. Most likely, your legal career will mean those times in your working life when your energies are devoted to legal issues. Some lawyers move in and out of law practice, alternating legal roles, family roles, and business roles, yet still having an internally understood, personal career path. Others reject any notion of career, seeing their opportunities as a succession of gigs that may or may not require a law license.

Before Law School

If you are already a lawyer, or about to graduate from law school, these next two sections may not apply to you. They are offered here for those considering a legal career.

Pick a Rigorous College Major

The best advice for a college student considering the law is to major in something serious. Intellectual challenge is more important than subject matter. Physics, history, English, or math can all provide a solid foundation for law school. These majors require rigorous critical thinking. Law is complex and analytical. It hones fine distinctions. It demands quick, precise thinking and writing. Any academic field that requires the brain to absorb complex ideas and then be able to express those ideas in succinct statements is good preparation for law school. Heavy-duty writing assignments sharpen both analysis and organization. The less analytical the discipline, the more challenging the student will find law school. Taking on a hard-core academic discipline and mastering it is the most effective way a college student can prepare for law school.

Take the LSAT Review Course Seriously

Today the LSAT weighs heavily as a factor in law school admission. When I took the LSAT, I prepared for the test the best way I knew how: I skipped my fraternity's Friday night party and went to bed early. I knew getting a good night's sleep would be important. That was the extent of my LSAT preparation. If there were LSAT prep courses then, I was unaware of them. Today, a good review course can add points to the score. But just taking the course doesn't rack up the extra points. The edge is gained by taking it seriously, as if it were another job. Attend every class, complete every exercise, do as much of the "extra" work as you can. Just a few more points can make the difference between admission to your dream school or one lower on your list.

Law School

Hiring Is Driven by Solving Problems

Each law school has its own culture and its own popular myths that some students embrace as revealed truths. For instance: good summer placements are essential; judicial clerkships are critical for a litigation career; and the kiss of death is not having a job lined up before graduation. The presumptive trajectory of a summer internship to a judicial clerkship to career success is not a guarantee, nor does the lack of it lead to a dead end. There are no guarantees. Securing a job during the second summer may indeed bring a job offer along with the added benefit of an anxiety-free third year, but not always. Fluctuations in the economy, the number of new graduates, and the number of experienced lawyers postponing retirement all affect what jobs are available for law students. There is no such thing as permanent employment or even a secure job. Everything changes all the time.

The real value of these summer experiences is to help students discern if they really want to do this kind of work. The summer intern needs to ask if these are the kinds of people she enjoys being around and if the opportunities this firm offers motivate her to produce her best work. Law school placement offices favor this model of progression from first summer job to second summer job to a clerkship to a job offer. They prefer it because it is the easiest way for placement offices to quantify, on paper, their effectiveness.[i] While this model may work for the top students, most law students still have to scramble. Depending on a law school placement office to secure the ideal job can prove to be an ineffective strategy. The school's career office may provide tools, suggestions, and introductions, but it is always the student's task to land the job. The earlier the law student grasps this, the easier the process will be.

Many law school myths are the result of crowdsourcing at its worst. Gossip mixed with third-hand rumor combines to form a body of inaccurate common knowledge about the profession and its practitioners. The news from legal blogs varies in quality and accuracy. Even the most perceptive observers of legal trends can offer only general advice as to which way the economic wind may be blowing when a student finally enters the job market. The result is that law students may be led into making significant career decisions based on community myth rather than rational analysis and personal desire. Even in hard times, some firms hire some lawyers. Lawyers are hired during market panics and at the bottom of depressions. In fact, there is never an impossible time to find a job; some years are just more difficult than others.

The challenge for law students, in good times and bad, is to ferret out the situations where their talent satisfies real needs. That is the key to a job offer. If the skill you can provide meets the need an employer has, an offer may follow. This is even true if a skill you project meets a need the employer only imagines. The fastest path to a job offer is the employer's seeing the applicant as a solution to an unresolved problem.

Long ago, I heard a podcast I have never forgotten. The speaker said that if job applicants can present themselves as the solution to the employer's problem, there will be a job offer. This holds true, he said, whether the company is "looking" for someone to hire or not. Law firms are no different. For those seeking legal jobs, the challenge is to figure out what the firm's problems are, so they can demonstrate how hiring them provides a solution. A law firm will not admit that the reason it has high turnover is one of its partners is difficult to work with and burns through associates. It may not want you to know that one of its key sections is failing and the firm needs to develop other areas of expertise. But basic internet research and network contacts can smoke this out. The law student who figures out the real reason a firm is hiring has a much better chance of receiving an offer. Without thorough research, going into an interview (or writing a cover letter and sending a resumé) is a waste of time.

Write a Resumé That Stands Out

As the initial foray into the job market, some placement offices recommend that students draft cover letters and resumés to be sent out to hiring firms. This traditional approach may work well for the top students, but for most others it becomes a huge frustration. The placement office may suggest a resumé template and most students – not knowing any better – dutifully follow it. The predictable result, of course, is that the resumés all tend to look the same. Grades and rank in class may be different (for those schools allowing disclosure of that information), but the awards, leadership positions, and volunteer experiences all merge into a fuzzy blob. Coveted award titles such as the "J. Franklin Doe Fellowship" conceal whatever honor the award was meant to confer. If a student's resumé looks the same as every other one, the chance of it generating any real interest is negligible. Resumés should present distinct individuals. Every law student will have grades and activities. What makes a resumé different is what makes the student different. The people who aren't impressed by the difference will not hire that student anyway, but the ones who are might want to meet the person behind the resumé.

Sometimes a placement office's advice is just wrong. Some years ago, I interviewed a law student solely because he had worked as a welder's assistant in a shipyard. I was looking for a lawyer who could help me in a management-side labor relations practice. I figured a former union-represented welder's assistant who went to law school could connect with working people. Of course, he had good grades and all the other quality markers, but it was his work experience I noticed. During the interview, I learned that his school's placement office had advised him to remove that welder's assistant job from his resumé.

They did not consider it to be "legal experience" and thought it did not fit on an application to a law firm. Well, it fit perfectly for me. I hired him.

Another time, I interviewed an applicant who had achieved the rank of Eagle Scout. That honor was not on his resumé. His placement office said any honors received in high school were not relevant to legal employment. Yet if young people can distinguish themselves early in life by receiving Scouting's highest award, how is that not relevant? Stars tend to keep on shining – and law firms want to hire stars.

The idea that a successful career in litigation first requires clerking for a court is also a myth. Judicial clerkships are valuable. If the lawyer intends to stay in the community, a clerkship with a local judge introduces her to court procedures from the inside and exposes her to the lawyers practicing at that bar. It is a solid way to gain knowledge and build relationships before embarking on a trial career. Yet a clerkship is not a prerequisite for a successful litigation career. Starting practice with a firm that has regular trial work exposes the new lawyer to the challenges of working with clients and navigating the court system from the bottom up. Getting to know local lawyers as colleagues avoids that awkwardness when the former clerk leaves the protective confines of chambers and enters the field of combat. There are distinct advantages to both. Law students should ask themselves if a clerkship is the best choice for what they want to do.

Either way, law students should take every opportunity to meet lawyers. More than general career guidance, what law students really need is hands-on, experienced mentors who listen to what they want to do and can advise them on how to achieve their goals. The best advice about practicing law comes from people who practice law.

First Job

The season immediately following the bar exam presents specific, but somewhat inconsistent, tasks. The first task, if you do not already have a job, is to find one. The second is to learn the rudiments of how to practice law. The third is to focus on becoming the lawyer you want to be even though you may not yet be in a job that will lead to your goal.

Meet and Network With Lawyers

There are many good resources on how to find a legal job. My own method is summed up in two words: meet lawyers. You can read books, visit websites, mail resumés, and fill out applications, but the most effective way to get a legal job is to meet lawyers. Join every bar association you can afford and go to its meetings, lunches, CLEs, and social events. Let every lawyer you meet know what you are looking for. Let everyone in your network of friends know you are available. None of the advances in modern technology has yet supplanted the process of lawyers hiring lawyers.

Learn How to Practice Law

For about the first five years, the lawyer's main task is to learn how to practice law. This initial process ends when the lawyer begins to have a feeling of internal confidence after beginning to see the same problems reappear. This transformation usually begins between the third and fifth year of practice, when the lawyer begins to feel more comfortable confronting new issues. The lawyer seems to know the next right steps to take and can converse with a client without fear of saying something stupid. Each new case is less mysterious. Even experienced lawyers know they are still just practicing the craft. There is always more to learn, new cases and rules to absorb, new personalities to accommodate. Anxiety still affects these accomplished practitioners; they just understand that the situation is seldom as dire or confusing as it appears to less experienced lawyers.

The hard truth is that the first years of law practice are difficult. Law practice presents a much different challenge than law school. This is especially true today when our profession is in the midst of transition in both technology and client expectations. Many lawyers in practice need a sophisticated understanding of how to analyze large quantities of data. Clients expect law firms to understand project management techniques to handle their transactional and litigation matters efficiently. Most new lawyers, not having learned these skills in school, will have to gain expertise on the job.

In law school, students are introduced to a way of organizing information that appears alien to what they may have learned in college. It is the rare student for whom the discipline of IRAC comes naturally. To brief a case in law school usually means to analyze given facts in relation to legal principles and then to articulate a court's reasoning behind its decision. In law practice, clients do not enter the lawyer's office with statements of fact. They come in with problems that may or may not have a legal solution.

Often, clients present incidents that are self-contradictory or wholly unconnected anywhere except in their own minds. The lawyer's task is to identify a legal theory that could offer the relief the client desires. Do the facts presented by the client contain the elements of any viable theory? Even if the lawyer discovers one promising theory, she should probably also find an alternative in case the first one crumbles under scrutiny. Once the theoretical alternatives are in place, the lawyer then needs to develop a strategy, the steps (legal and non-legal) most likely to deliver the desired result.

So, what the lawyer does in practice is precisely the reverse of what he learned to do as a law student. Law students analyze theories of court decisions based on given facts. Lawyers seek data from a client's story to support factual elements of potential legal theories. Since the introduction of clinical courses in law school, this process has become more familiar to law students. Nonetheless, the study of appellate cases still forms the backbone of law school training. It should come as no surprise, then, that the transition from law school to law practice is a bumpy road. Even the most accomplished law student experiences some frustration and discouragement in the first years of practice.

Every year, associates in many firms receive their annual reviews. I will never forget one of my first reviews. At that time, the larger firms were transitioning from the expectation that if associates did good work and kept out of trouble, they would be made partner – as opposed to the more current, more selective "up or out" model. Thus, it became important that the associate be criticized for some deficiency in every review, so there would be a record on which to base an "out" decision if that was the firm's later conclusion. In one memorable review, I was upbraided for not being "fully committed" to the firm. I had undertaken some significant charitable and civic obligations that I believed were important components of a legal career. What I heard in the review was, "JB, you're spending a lot of time on outside interests – time we believe would be better spent working in the firm, like Todd[ii] does." I kept quiet, stifling the urge to remind the three partners that while my friend Todd was certainly a hard worker, I had never billed less than 2000 hours a year on client matters.

I walked glumly back to my office, passing Todd in the hall on the way to his review. "Wish me luck," he said as I turned into my office. One half-hour later, Todd stormed into my office, sputtering, "I've been working my butt off for this place, and can you imagine what they told me?" "I can't imagine," I replied sarcastically. "They didn't say a word about my billable hours," complained Todd. "They said, 'Why aren't you getting out in the community like JB is?'"

Takeaway Tips

Pick a rigorous college major
Treat the LSAT review course like a job
Remember that hiring is driven by problems that need to be solved
Write a resumé that stands out
Meet and network with lawyers
Learn how to practice law.

Notes

i Law school placement statistics are inherently suspect. Some law schools are now subsidizing jobs for recent graduates to artificially inflate their post-graduation employment numbers. Most calculations also include temporary jobs (such as legal clerkships), part-time jobs, and jobs not requiring a law degree.

ii All names of individuals have been changed to protect privacy.

CHAPTER II

Transitioning Into Practice

Before transitioning from school to practice, new lawyers have two major challenges: passing the bar and finding employment. During the first two years of law school, most students obsess about grades. But then, in the third year, their eyes turn to the bar exam. Since a great majority of law graduates pass the bar exam, the obsession seems over-hyped. The bar exam, however, is the line that separates licensed lawyers from law school graduates. It's non-negotiable and must be taken seriously.

Take a Bar-Prep Course

Law school has its own defined tasks (courses), schedules (semesters) and evaluations (grades). If the student completes the requirements, he receives a degree. For the student who wants to be a lawyer, the degree is the ticket to the bar exam – nothing more, nothing less. The bar exam is unconnected with either law school or law practice. It is a timed test measuring whether the student can apply legal concepts to a limited set of fact patterns. The bar exam is only the gate through which the student must pass to become a licensed practitioner. It may provide an amusing source of anecdotes for the future but, beyond licensure, it has no practical utility. Currently there are forces pushing to end bar exams, but in all likelihood, they will persist for some time.

The bar examination is only tangentially related to what students learn in law school. It tests understanding of some legal concepts presented in law school, especially as they relate to the state giving the exam. It also tests whether a student can spot legal issues. The multijurisdictional questions are directed more toward eliminating wrong answers in a compressed time frame than elucidating broad principles. In short, the bar exam is a trivia game most contestants win. Fortunately, bar review courses teach the test rather than the law. They show students the tricks to beat the game. They make no pretense of teaching law. So, if the principle the review course teaches contradicts a favorite professor's strongly held view, the review course's approach is more likely to be the correct answer.

DOI: 10.4324/9781003533672-3

The student is well advised to follow the direction and pace of the review course. Review courses are designed to have the student's preparation peak at the very time they take the exam. Thus, it is important to stay well within the bounds prescribed by the course. Working ahead or lagging behind can have negative results. Staying in the middle of the pack, difficult as it may be for many law students, is the prime position for success. The highest and lowest passing grades earn the same license. Every year, some students fail the exam because they are just tired of law school and want to give themselves a break. Bar preparation requires being all in, all the time. The break comes later.

One of the ironies of our profession is that, although admission to a better school may result in access to more desirable jobs, all lawyers end up with the same license. The highest-scoring bar applicant's license grants the same privileges as the lowest-scoring. The bar exam ignores schools, grades, and honors. The student who was not admitted to the prestigious law school and didn't make law review – but passed the bar – can have a legal career limited only by ingenuity and effort. That first job may not ooze prestige, but with persistence, new lawyers can build the clientele, the practice, and the career they dreamed of.

A lawyer's career is the lawyer's responsibility. From the very start, students and new lawyers need to be proactive about their own careers. Your vision and your goals belong to you. Advice may be helpful, but it is never a substitute for your own internal compass.

Think Serving, Not Training

The transition from law school to law practice requires a fundamental shift in mindset. The purpose of law school is to introduce the craft of legal analysis, thinking, and writing, so the student is able to "think like a lawyer" and prepared to take a bar exam to become a licensed member of the profession. Law school is student centric. It succeeds when the student passes the bar and is ready for the transformation to professional status. For three years the spotlight has been on the student; the school's efforts are concentrated on helping students succeed.

Law practice, however, is client centric. Practicing lawyers help clients achieve client goals, not their own. The client's desires, even when misguided, always hold center stage. The primary internal shift the new lawyer needs to make is from expecting to be served by a law school to becoming an instrument of service to clients.

Sometimes the tasks law students and new lawyers perform seem similar – for instance, doing legal research and writing a memorandum. If a thorny issue arises, the student assumes she can ask the professor, knowing questions are expected. Supervisors, too, expect and welcome questions. But not having considered a particular legal issue for some time, supervisors expect the associate first to have researched the area before forming the question. Legal memoranda in law practice are not teaching tools; they are the building blocks of legal advice. Questions directed to a professor might initiate a complete Socratic dialogue. Law practice supervisors, thoroughly familiar with Socratic questioning, expect questions from associates to directly address the assigned task. Speculative legal theory that doesn't affect the case is not as valued as it was in law school.

Thus, expectations differ between law school professors and law firm supervisors. Professors expect that the assigned material is learned, absorbed, and thoroughly understood. Law school papers and tests are designed to evaluate how well this has been achieved. A firm supervisor's assignment has a different purpose. It is designed to provide legal advice, upon which the client may make a decision, act, or do nothing at all. Clients seek legal advice to understand the choices available to them in disputes or transactions. Legal research, then, is not an abstract exercise but one of the essential components of a client decision.

For many students, this transition is made easier by having spent time working in law firms, either as a summer associate or as a part-time employee during the school year. A student's work in a law firm may range from legal research to running errands. Students can experience firsthand the cumbersome process of transforming legal research into arguments and then into briefs to be filed in court. Students also learn that even though courts may have the same rules, the process of filing may be different based on a local judge's preferences. Pleadings do not magically file themselves with the clerk of court; someone needs to deliver them in the correct format, to the right place, at the right time. In the analog days of practice, there was a physicality of document production – printing, collating, stapling, and delivering – a process that lawyers needed to master because there was no guarantee that anyone else would be available to do it. Likewise, today's lawyers need to be master PDF manipulators and electronic filing gurus. Law students lucky enough to get these experiences will have more insight into what a firm expects. But once hired as a lawyer, the former student discerns the stakes are high and the firm's expectations are higher.

Every law firm, legal clinic, and corporate law department has a budget. A firm's minimal expectation is to at least break even on every new lawyer hired. As the lawyer progresses, the firm intends to reap a substantial profit from them. So, regardless of the level of the first-year salary, the firm intends to recapture every nickel of it. Students pay law schools. Law practices pay lawyers. Misunderstanding this fundamental equation may lead new associates into believing their role is to receive training rather than to provide service. In a for-profit legal organization, any training received is only incidental to the service provided. In a non-profit, resources are even scarcer, and effective use of lawyer time conserves those resources to provide more efficient client service.

Prepare for Different Expectations

Law practice tasks are the problems clients present or the assignments supervising lawyers give. Schedules are statutory deadlines, court deadlines, or supervisor-imposed deadlines. There is no one form of evaluation. Some supervisor evaluations are highly idiosyncratic. Jobs otherwise well done may be evaluated poorly; likewise, marginal performance may induce plaudits. There is no grading curve. Indicators of success may include fees paid promptly, pay raises, bonuses, client referrals, professional advancement, or an invitation to partnership. Lawyer success is measured by results, not numbers or words.

In law practice, every matter includes moving targets. Each case or transaction has its own internal tasks and schedules that change, often with little notice, based on client, adversary, or tribunal decisions. Supervisor assignments then become a form of triage to focus the organization's best resources on its most critical problems at a moment in time. Priorities may be reshuffled, even within the same day. Lawyers immersed in trial preparation may, after one phone call, discover their case has settled and they have little on their schedule for the next three weeks. Long-term, constant working on projects that may either evaporate or explode teaches the lawyer to quickly switch gears. Otherwise, it takes a toll on the lawyer's health and attitude.

Most of the time, the assigning lawyer already knows the broad outlines of the law. Their questions are based on a body of legal knowledge with which they are already familiar. The assigning lawyer may tell the novice where that knowledge is to be found and may present a narrowly honed research question, so the research is more focused on the goal. An effective assigning lawyer warns about dead ends, those paths of research that may seem promising but have proven fruitless. Often the assigning lawyer may think he already knows the answer to the question but needs to be sure his conclusion is based on the latest law rather than his own fallible recollection. In short, the functional difference between law school and law firm research projects is the difference between teaching the student and advising the client. Firm research, unlike class assignments, has economic consequences.

When you start a new job, your employer assumes that your first priority will be to perform the job up to expectations. You will work more hours than you want; you will sacrifice leisure and family time to complete firm projects. Full days off may be rare. While this contradicts the current emphasis on work/life balance, putting work first at the start of a career accelerates it toward the success you desire. Remember, you are in this for the long term.

Network to Find a Job

After passing the bar, the student's next task is to secure a job, if they have not already been offered one. Many students depend on their law school's placement office to guide them to their first legal job. This is short-sighted. The national law school ranking lists put a high value on the first job out of school as a factor in that school's ranking. The percentage of graduating students who have jobs upon graduation affects the law school's ranking compared to other schools. So, since ranking seems to have become all-important for law schools, many of them are creating jobs for their most recent graduates to raise their percentages in post-school placements – and thus enhance their school's ranking. These jobs may be internships or pro bono opportunities, but what they share is the lack of a clear path to sustained employment. While these placeholder jobs inflate employment numbers for the law school, the graduate must still find employment after the placement's term has ended. The new lawyer's problem is postponed rather than solved.

Relentless networking makes finding a legal job much easier. Local and state bar associations often provide free or reduced cost memberships for law students and new lawyers. Becoming active in those associations exposes students and new lawyers to people who can help them or hire them, either on a project basis or to fill a need within a firm. Just getting to know more lawyers creates broader networks for the law student. Word-of-mouth opens doors. Experienced lawyers learning about job opportunities may pass those nuggets on to the new lawyers they know. They may know of a firm's needs the new lawyer could fill, whether that firm has advertised an opening or not.

It is easy to get discouraged when looking for a job, but persistence is key. A former student of mine had a dream of becoming an environmental lawyer. He joined the ABA environmental section as a law student. He bounced around several small firms in his home state doing tort defense work but kept his memberships and his environmental law dream alive. He talked about it every chance he got and wrote articles for any publication that would take them. Slowly, he began to attract some environmental cases, and today he leads his state's largest independent environmental protection group. He refused to let his dream die and, ultimately, it took wings. The dedication it takes to complete law school and pass the bar is sufficient to turn a dream into a reality.

Face New Challenges Head On

After I passed the bar and found a job in a firm, my first months as a lawyer were spent learning how to perform tasks I had never been introduced to in law school. Some were rote, like learning how to keep loose-leaf subscription services up to date (one of many tasks the digital world has thankfully obliterated). Other responsibilities, like learning how to take a simple deposition, were more subtle and required the integration of law school skills, assessing facts, finding gaps in evidence, and asking pointed questions. Pulled together, these formed the outline for a deposition.

My first labor negotiation struck fear in my heart. I had never done anything like it before. In this case, the union and the company had a long history of hostile relations. I was told I was going to be meeting with the union to arrange some mid-contract changes in the labor agreement. Just hearing that I was going to be the company's lead negotiator (in fact, the company's only negotiator) set off all my internal alarms.

In my labor law class, I learned that any verbal misstep in a union negotiation could result in the company's being charged with an unfair labor practice. I had sat in on a couple of negotiating sessions, but I had never taken the lead in one. My boss assured me this would be easy. Easy for him, I thought.

Conceptually, the assignment was simple. The country was in the middle of escalating inflation and prices were rising faster than wages, making it more attractive for workers to change jobs, even union-represented jobs, than to remain in the job they had. My task was to schedule a meeting with the union representatives and get them to agree to a mid-contract wage increase. In other words, the contract wage was already set, and my assignment was to get the union to agree to accept more money per hour than the contract already provided. Unsurprisingly, it went off without a hitch. The union was delighted to accept more money. Smiles and handshakes all around. I exhaled.

From my perspective today, this was the easiest labor negotiation imaginable. But it felt very different at the time. I was in an unknown territory. I was expected to accomplish a goal I had never before attempted, dealing with people I did not know, on legal grounds full of landmines. And this turned out to be just one of many first experiences I survived during that first year. All of us will have early experiences like this. Success will come from facing the new challenge head-on. Break it down into its component parts: identify a clear goal, research the law, check up on the adversaries, and develop a planned approach. While the entire task may appear formidable, each of the parts is within our capacity. Knowing that builds our confidence to take on the challenge.

Record Time Accurately

Law students don't usually account for the time they spend on each project. Billing by the hour, however, is still common in law firms. Many new lawyers are uncomfortable accurately recording the amount of time they spend completing a project. They assume that because of their inexperience, they are taking too long and thus they may understate their hours to make them look more efficient. Firms set billing rates for new lawyers knowing that it takes them longer to produce work. Under-reporting hours worked is detrimental to the new lawyer because a record of low hours indicates either low productivity or the availability to do more work. Understating hours also distorts the supervisor's view of the difficulty of an assignment and the value of the work the new lawyer produced. Thus, under-reporting hours hurts both the new lawyer and the firm.

Billing lawyers have an ethical duty to present bills that are complete and fair. If time needs to be cut, that is the job of the billing attorney, not the new lawyer. The new lawyer's main concern is to get the assignment right. In the long run, the hours recorded will take care of themselves. My first boss made the point quite clearly when I told him how embarrassed I felt to have spent so much time on a simple project. He responded, "Why do you think we bill you so cheap?"

Takeaway Tips

Take a bar prep course
Think serving, not training
Prepare for different expectations
Network to find a job
Face new challenges head on
Record time accurately.

CHAPTER III

Advancing Your Career

One of the first things many new associates want to know is how long it will take the firm to make them a partner. This is the wrong question. Firms do not just "make" anyone a partner; lawyers are invited into a partnership when the firm determines it has more to lose if the lawyers leave than if they are admitted into the partnership. In other words, lawyers earn the right to stay in a firm; they may even earn the right to participate in its profits. If, however, they are encouraged to leave, it is because the firm saw a better economic opportunity by their departure than by their retention. Law firms have developed many creative categories that appear to be promotions, and may even offer higher salaries or bonus opportunities, but fall short of participation in the equity structure of the firm. Non-equity partners may be essential to maintain depth of coverage in a firm's areas of practice, but they remain employees, not owners.

Make Money for the Firm

Effective law firms behave rationally. Decisions about what lawyers a firm needs to keep are based on economics, not sentiment. Firms advance lawyers when they need to, when any other alternative is less beneficial than the promotion. Some firms still maintain that "under normal circumstances, there is a seven-to-ten-year track to partner." It would be intemperate to call this a flat-out lie, but it plainly shades the truth. Firms take on new equity participants only when that choice best suits their own interests, not before.

Thus, the path to success within a firm is for the lawyer to become a critical component of that firm's business.

Generally, this happens in two ways. The first is the associate who learns the lawyer's craft and becomes skilled in developing client relationships. As a new lawyer, she will begin by doing work assigned by the firm. But as she develops valuable skills, she may become important in keeping the firm's regular clients satisfied, and she may begin attracting new ones on her own. Even if she does not develop a rainmaker reputation, the firm counts on her to continue to build their practice. The second path to success is to become an expert in a legal specialty the firm needs to either serve its existing clients or attract new

 DOI: 10.4324/9781003533672-4

ones. While this lawyer may never grow the firm's client base, she is, nonetheless, essential to the firm's long-term success – at least until the firm finds a lawyer with the same legal expertise coupled with the ability to attract new clients. Each of these lawyers will be encouraged to stay.

Some firms even claim to lose money on new lawyers. Generally, that is not true; they just do not make as much as later, when the lawyer gains more experience. If it costs a firm $200,000 a year (salary plus overhead costs and benefits) to support a new lawyer and the lawyer bills 1600 hours a year, the firm breaks even if the lawyer realizes $125 for each hour billed. That is not a large number at this level of cost. Higher salaries, benefits, and costs require an even higher realized rate. Even charitable organizations expect a gain for any hire they make. Law firms expect profit.

When recruiting a new associate, the law firm representative may offer career encouragement such as, "We'll help you develop as a lawyer," or "You'll get great mentoring here." But the new lawyer must never forget she was hired because the firm needed tasks performed. One of the privileges of law practice is the opportunity to learn new things every day. This, however, is a by-product of producing legal work, not its purpose. The purpose is to serve the client, not satisfy the lawyer's curiosity. Here is another example where law practice differs from law school. The purpose of student questions is to better understand the law and its exceptions. Lawyer questions tend to be more focused: how particular facts or theories affect achieving a client's goal. Law firms seek to achieve client goals, not simply respond to abstract questions.

Appreciate Law's Unique Culture

Unlike some professions where those at the top discount what new members can contribute, seasoned lawyers absolutely depend upon new lawyers. New lawyers do the basic legal research and write memos outlining the law. These form the basis of legal advice to important clients. Experienced lawyers, since they did this work themselves when they entered the profession, know where an analysis is incomplete or where the research jumped the track. The result is a legal culture wherein senior lawyers respect their less experienced colleagues because they depend on them. They appreciate the independent intelligence new lawyers bring, even if it hasn't yet been fully formed by years of practice. When a legal team debates which theory will be most successful, the junior lawyers are valued participants in the conversation. They are free to challenge or contradict those with more experience. After all, they are the ones who last read the cases and statutes.

Here, legal culture departs from business culture. A friend of mine described to me her experience as the most junior associate at a "closing dinner" in New York where clients and lawyers celebrated the consummation of a deal. The lawyers were seated with the most senior in the center, flanked by lawyers in order of descending seniority on each side. On the other side of the table, the client's officers were seated in the same respective order. When the client's CEO made a pithy observation, everyone else on his team would nod and dutifully agree with his insight. But when the senior partner of the law firm said something my junior associate friend thought was inaccurate, she chimed in with an alternate, more accurate explanation. The business team blanched at this breach of corporate etiquette. A subordinate had the nerve to contradict her boss. The lawyers, however, seemed not to notice anything unusual. A few even echoed the associate's thinking. This is just how lawyers interact with each other. The new lawyer's duty is to protect her boss from embarrassing the firm. Open disputation is part of our legal culture. Rather than having committed a career-ending offense, my friend proved herself to be a valuable player who protected her team.

Choose Two Good Mentors

Every new lawyer needs some good mentors. This is true whether the lawyer practices alone or in a group. But finding good mentors can be something of a minefield. Good mentors are willing to take time to show the new lawyer how to succeed in the workplace. Good mentors are willing to listen to whatever career questions come up, take them seriously, and give the new lawyer frank answers and a safe space to air concerns. They keep confidences. Good mentors are transparent; they share their own failures and challenges and reflect on what they could have done better. Accessibility, openness, honesty, and encouragement are the foundation of good mentorship.

While the range of mentor styles is as broad as the range of mentor personalities, ideally, the new lawyer should have at least two mentors. One would be inside the employing organization and the other outside. An internal mentor introduces the new lawyer to the ways the organization wants things done and its invisible traditions as well as diffusing the new lawyer's normal anxiety and fear of failure. The experience level of the internal mentor can extend from being a senior associate to a senior partner. Qualifications of an internal mentor are respect within the organization, time available to do the job, an understanding of the organization's culture and a willingness to share that knowledge. A successful mentor relationship is almost guaranteed if the internal mentor honestly cares about the new lawyer's professional development to the extent of becoming a willing sounding board and advocate within the firm. Unless the internal mentor is assigned by a firm mentor program, the new lawyer is wise to hold back from approaching a potential mentor until the new lawyer is convinced he wants what the potential mentor has to give.

While the new lawyer may find the ideal mentor through an internal firm program, that is not always the case. Effective mentorship depends on personal compatibility, safety of confidences and lack of an agenda beyond helping the new lawyer. If the assigned mentor is incompatible, the associate should find a trustworthy person within the firm to fulfill the role. Even in a profession where confidentiality is paramount, the new lawyer must always be wary of what is shared with any other firm lawyer. A lawyer's arrival, success, and departure have economic consequences for the organization. So, there is an inherent conflict of interest any time an associate's own career plans are inconsistent with the firm's plans for the associate.

Good external mentors are essential. They offer confidentiality and encouragement unfettered by firm loyalties that may color answers to questions about career advancement and personal goals. External mentors can offer a different perspective about the possibilities they see for the new lawyer's developing career.

Early in my own career, I met a lawyer at church who flung open a door I was afraid to even nudge. Clark and I had talked casually about law practice over the years. He had referred some cases to me. Sometimes we had lunch together, but mostly we saw each other at church. He was a general practitioner with a small firm and had the gift of tenacity. One Sunday during coffee hour, I was hesitantly broaching the idea that I might not want to spend my entire career with a big firm. The operative myth of my firm was that outside its walls there was really no law practice worth having. Any move away from the firm would be a step down – far down. Clark listened patiently but remained silent. I remember him balancing his coffee cup in his hands. When I came to the end of my ramblings, Clark looked me straight in the eye and, in a few words, kicked down the walls I had built around my own ambitions. "JB," he said, "did it ever occur to you that the firm doesn't own you?" I stood there surprised, shaken and a little humiliated. Clark had identified the extent to which I had given up my own dreams for a law firm's convenience. I felt as if Clark were standing there reading me my own, personal Emancipation Proclamation. He had given me permission to follow my heart. I don't know why I needed that permission, but Clark gave it. A few weeks later, I was in the process of forming my own firm with two partners, and I never looked back.

The agenda of mentorship, whether internal or external, is straightforward. It is to introduce the culture and expectations of the profession, the community, and the organizations served while encouraging the new lawyer's efforts to learn to practice law. The mentor explains community standards, such as civility in all things. The mentee is free to ask any question at all. Each mentor/mentee relationship will be different based on the interests, aptitudes, and concerns of both mentor and mentee. Good mentorship is not indoctrination. The mentee can take or leave what is being offered. Mentors can offer what they believe to be important, whether their colleagues agree or not. In this sense, good mentoring is highly idiosyncratic. It's a personal relationship, not a transaction. While there are no fixed boundaries, the focus is on the development of the new lawyer. The corollary benefit for that new lawyer is finding an ally in a more experienced member of the bar. The benefit for the mentor is staying in touch with the new generation's perspective as well as making a new friend.

Personal Development

When I was an associate in a large law firm, I remember a friend telling me that a partner at a rival firm referred to his associates as FBUs: Fungible Billing Units. He saw them just as costs on a balance sheet expected to produce some multiple of their salaries. Whether they stayed or left was, to him, irrelevant. What counted was the firm's bottom line. There may be some lawyers who think that way. But even they are not as dangerous as the new lawyers who adopt the belief that their only independent worth is measured by their billable hours. Working in a large organization, it is easy for the new lawyer to convince herself of her expendability. Making her own mark and attracting her own clients may seem far out of reach. The danger is that if she believes this is true, it probably is. The remedy is to stay focused on your own long-term goals.

Develop Your Own Style

From the outset, we have the choice to fit in and not make waves or to push ourselves to develop our own best abilities. Once we become competent in the basics, we can then adjust our work pattern to suit our own personality. When we are finally adept at everything the job requires, we can integrate what we have learned about practicing law with our own personal way of getting things done. It is this integration that frees our best abilities and unleashes our signature style. Every lawyer who practices at a high level of professional competence has a personal way of doing it. While earlier in our career, we may have mimicked senior lawyers to become the lawyer they wanted us to become, ultimately, to be fully successful, we need to become a lawyer empowered through our own personality and skills. First, learn to do the job the way your supervisor wants it done, and having mastered that, do it the way you know best.

There is more than one right way to accomplish a task. At the outset, the associate learns the discipline of doing it the way the supervisor knows it will succeed. The experience is even richer when working for different supervisors who have different preferences and styles. The associate who masters this is well on the way to developing his own best practices.

Current parlance refers to this development of skills, personal habits, and style as "branding." We begin developing our brand from the day we start; eventually, it becomes the way we are known within the profession. Our areas of expertise, how we engender trust, how we approach a case, and how we behave during conflict all combine to set us apart as professionals with a distinctive style. Our task is to ensure the style we are developing supports the goals we have set to achieve.

Internal conflict arises when our firm wants us to develop in a way that is inconsistent with our brand. For example, a lawyer known for involvement in civic affairs will feel squeezed when the firm wants 400 more billable hours by the end of the year. The lawyer will feel that long-term relationship building is suffering from the firm's short-term desire for more revenue. The cost of attempting to achieve both may be falling short in some other area of life, resulting in a loss of enthusiasm for the firm and for the practice of law.

The modern law firm is ruthless. While its administration may articulate goals about lawyer well-being, work/life balance, or pro bono engagement, management always has its eye on the bottom line: profit per lawyer. This may prove inconsistent with the lawyer's own life-plan, and the time may come when there is a clear choice between the role the lawyer wants the practice to play in life and the role the firm expects. While it may not feel like it at the time, the lawyer always has a choice.

Short-term thinking does not produce great lawyers. Some of today's most important businesses did not exist 10 or 20 years ago. Significant enterprises are being formed by people only a few years out of college – or those who dropped out. A firm's point of contact for its largest clients will seldom be a new lawyer. But new lawyers can develop relationships with the new generation of leaders and become points of contact for businesses that will, in the future, become important clients. The legendary giants of firms past have died. Their replacements have retired. Mortality always favors the new lawyer. Within one generation, most firms, as well as their clients, will have changed leadership several times, so taking the long view, there is always opportunity for those who seek it.

The first time I heard the term "golden handcuffs" was from my friend Bob, a partner in a large southeastern law firm. A Harvard law graduate, Bob had a quick intelligence and an incisive tongue. He asserted his own style from his first day at work. He had the ability to cut to the heart of a case and negotiate an elegant solution. This gave him some protection from the conflict between his freewheeling style and the firm's conservative culture. Bob had many opportunities to move his practice elsewhere or to start his own boutique, but he stayed at the firm for his entire career. He said it was the golden handcuffs. They paid him too much to give him any incentive to leave. Personally, I think he enjoyed being the plaid sport jacket lawyer in a firm of custom suits. For Bob, golden handcuffs were a lighthearted excuse. For other lawyers, however, they may be just handcuffs.

What turns the gold into handcuffs is subtle. We buy a house that is larger and more expensive than our family needs. We sign our children up for private schools, join country clubs, and buy a vacation house. Soon there is little gap between our income and our lifestyle. Credit cards balance everything out. A lawyer following this path has wandered out on thin ice. Career decisions have then been made by the need to maintain a lifestyle rather than by staying true to the lawyer's own desires.

Firms know this. Some even subconsciously encourage lawyers to live on the edge, figuring it ensures dedication to the firm. Partner comments such as "You can't do better anywhere else" or "We are the real lawyers here" reinforce the message. The result is a trap that obscures a lawyer's vision. We begin to think if we leave Big, Bigger, and Biggest, we will fail. We think we need to stay here because we really can't do better anywhere else. We think we need the money, and it might be too risky to make a change. Thus, we deprive ourselves of the power to choose and slip those handcuffs on our own wrists.

This false reasoning may never surface far enough to allow conscious analysis. But lying just below the surface of our awareness, this nascent thought limits our ability to choose what is best for us. We retain our power to choose by retaining a sense of who we are as a lawyer. We refuse to let a firm define who we will become. We can be a great team player without turning our autonomy over to the team. Our talent can survive a change of employment. Long term, the lawyers with successful careers are the ones who live below their means, not beyond them. They have the stability to take a risk, make a change, or stay on their chosen path.

Passages

It was December 1979 and I had been with the firm six years. It was the night of the annual Christmas party held at a prestigious country club. Going to that country club always made me nervous. It was where the first families played in the summer and partied in the winter. It exuded an ambiguous welcome. The polite greetings of uniformed retainers belied the underlying tone of condescension. They knew we were not members; we were contingently welcome. We could visit but not stay.

Groups of lawyers and their spouses clustered, and my wife and I found a cluster of friends to greet. There was an open bar in every corner of the room; drinks appeared quickly and were poured liberally. A large poster board set up next to an enormous Christmas tree displayed childhood photos of this year's crop of newly made partners. It suggested that while you may feel very important now – as a new partner – once you were not so exalted; you were just a kid like we all once were.

At dinner, my wife and I sat at a table with two other couples. One husband was an associate like me, the other a partner. The partner's wife looked at me with dull, lifeless eyes and told me how secure she felt that her husband was a partner in such a great firm. "George is a partner now, so I guess we have it made," she said.

After dinner, before the dancing began, the organizers had planned a skit for entertainment. It was parody of firm life from the perspective of the wives. Back then, the lawyers, save one, were all men and the spouses, all women. The crowd loved the skit. The laughter and playful hoots were almost constant. I don't remember anything about the script of the skit or any of the lines everyone else thought were so funny. For some reason, I couldn't take in what was being presented in front of me. I couldn't grasp the words. I could only hear the subtext, the feelings under the words. And what I heard felt like a punch in the gut: "I love you, but I never see you." "You missed your daughter's birthday party." "Your children don't know who you are anymore." "I'm scared and lonely." Those messages came across clearly, but no one else seemed to be on tuned in to my channel. I looked across the table and saw my wife, a happy, animated, enthusiastic person. She wasn't laughing either. In fact, she looked rather grim.

When the skit ended and the dancing was to begin, I took my wife's hand, and we walked over to the Christmas tree and the poster with all the photos. We looked at the photos and then back at the large group freshening their drinks and getting ready to party. "We're out of here," I said. Together we walked in silence to the car. Before we got in, my wife turned to me and said, "Yes, we're out of here."

Decide When It's Time to Move On

No matter how the new lawyer begins her career, she must not take a passive stance toward her advancement. From the first day of employment, the new lawyer should ask, "Do I want to tie my economic and professional future to this organization?" Perhaps the only reason she joined the firm was to gain experience in a field of law, to work with an outstanding mentor, or to beef up her resumé for the next job. In that case, she needs to set some decision points where she asks herself if her goals in taking this job have been met. If so, is it time to move on?

Goals evolve over time, and the job may have opened opportunities that became more attractive than the lawyer's original plan. This could be a good reason to stay with the firm and turn those opportunities into a viable law practice. It is not uncommon, however, for the lawyer to feel she is in a rut, producing the good work the partners want, but not advancing as a lawyer herself, either in terms of achievement or reputation. This is a tough call: to stay or to go. Staying usually appears to be the safe bet, but it may not be the wise one. When the associate gets what he came for and the opportunity ahead seems to be limited to working more hours and making more money, it may be time to leave.

It would be nice if there were a clear formula telling the lawyer when it is time to leave. The answer lies in the intersection of what the present employer can offer and what the lawyer needs to advance or transform his career. If the current employer offers a path in which the lawyer can be satisfied by developing a practice and meeting his goals, then remaining in place may be the best option. But if his current role feels like a dead end, it is probably time to go. Ultimately, this is a personal decision best made through honest introspection and discussion with trusted friends.

I have left three law firms for three different reasons, each reason appropriate for where I was on my own journey at the time. When I was 33, I left a large law firm because the person the firm wanted me to become was not the person I thought I was created to be. Yet it was a great law firm where I learned how to be a lawyer. I co-founded the second firm, which eventually grew to include over 20 lawyers. But I stayed there too long. I only left when it became obvious, even to me, that we were a collection of practices and lawyers without any common vision or goal. The third time I left a firm was when my son, an associate at that firm, wanted to start his own practice. So, I left and joined him in his new practice. I had come full circle. Once again, I was an associate in a law firm. Each decision to leave was difficult, but each transition offered new opportunities.

If remaining with a firm is still the goal, the lawyer needs to pay close attention to the firm's decisions. Law practice is dynamic. The direction of the general economy will enhance opportunities in some areas and reduce others. The lawyer who intends to remain and become a significant part of a law firm needs to keep an eye on two things. First, she needs to assure herself that the firm's leadership is attuned to changes in the culture and the economy. The firm needs to be positioned to prosper in a dynamic environment. Second, she needs to figure out where her own area of expertise has the greatest potential to thrive. She needs to sharpen her skills to catch that new growth. No area of law is immune to disruption. A successful career in a law firm today requires both a perceptive lawyer and a forward-looking firm. The firms that flourish tend to be those ready to turn disruptions into opportunities.

There are more choices for the new lawyer today than ever before. The pace of change is accelerating faster than some legal organizations can adapt. Law practice is in a process of radical deconstruction. The democratization of legal information means that anyone with a cell phone has access to cases, statutes, and regulations that, only a generation ago, were confined to books within the walls of law libraries. The next generation of lawyers will see the boundaries of law practice shrink even more as businesses use services that combine legal information with artificial intelligence to provide the legal advice once available only from licensed attorneys.

New lawyers need to be aware that the profession they are entering will look very different before their careers are half over. Flexibility will be essential to succeed in a profession that is in the process of re-definition. Clinging to the past is not a strategy for future success. The shelf life of the status quo keeps getting shorter. While no one has a clear view of what the future holds, those who keep an eye on the big picture will enjoy the competitive advantage.

Moments come in every lawyer's career when that lawyer must decide whether this job situation provides the path to the future she wants or whether she needs to make a change. There is no one test that provides the right answer. People leave jobs for all kinds of reasons: unrealistic expectations, lack of respect, lack of challenge, or simply boredom. Compensation is seldom a motivating reason because market forces tend to make salaries competitive.

When I entered the profession, there was the expectation that if you joined a good firm, did good work, and kept out of trouble, you would become an equity partner and stay with the same firm for your entire career. I don't know if that was an accurate assessment at the time, but things soon changed. The profession became more competitive, clients wanted fewer lawyers on cases, and profit per partner looked better when there were fewer partners. Lawyers starting out at a firm could not expect to be there for the duration of their careers. Firm cultures changed, anticipating that lawyers would move on and even equity partners or their whole teams would migrate among firms or launch independent practices.

Even if we perfectly understood the social and economic forces behind these changes, it would not answer the fundamental question every lawyer must confront at each step of a career. Who am I as a lawyer? What do I want to do? Who do I want to be? These are personal questions and must be approached as such. The lawyer who just cruises along and allows the professional self to be defined by the firm may have a good career. There is nothing dishonorable in this approach. But that lawyer never achieves dreams – in fact, that lawyer may never even allow dreams. That lawyer will always contribute less because he never unleashed his passion and used it.

The law asks too much to be taken casually. So, for lawyers who are totally committed to being lawyers, there is no substitute for knowing what they want, both from their lives and from their careers. Revisiting these questions at different points in a career may produce different answers. But the value is in continuing to ask the questions.

Takeaway Tips

Make money for the firm
Appreciate Law's unique culture
Choose two good mentors
Develop your own style
Decide when it's time to move on.

CHAPTER IV

Mastering Basic Skills

The time-honored lore of our profession suggests it takes about five years for the new lawyer to become grounded and achieve a sense of confidence. While this may not be an accurate measure, it is not debatable that the mastery of fundamental skills requires time in practice. To accelerate this process, the new lawyer is wise to think about gaining these skills from the outset rather than expecting to wake up one day and discover they are in place.

Work With Purpose

The place to start is to work with purpose. If we begin our work solely to get a couple of projects started or finished, we may accomplish that. But if that is all we do, we will fall short. If our purpose is to become a competent lawyer and build a practice or a career, and we approach the tasks of each day with that purpose in mind, we will accomplish much more. Considering how each work-day can advance our purpose offers a double benefit for the same effort. We approach each task as both a job to be finished and an opportunity to perfect our craft. If we work with our purpose in the back of our mind, regardless of the immediate task, we have a better chance of making that dream come true.

Seek Advice From Colleagues

Every court, agency, or office has its own unwritten rules and unarticulated expectations. One of my painful memories is standing outside a crowded courtroom with a client who was holding her small, crying baby. We were the last case on the docket, and I did everything I could think of to make the mother and baby comfortable. Everything, that is, except ask any of the court regulars for advice. When our case was finally called, the judge's clerk asked me, "Why didn't you let us know there was a baby waiting? We would have moved you up to the front." What I had thought to be my confidence showed itself to be my arrogance. I thought I did not need help. I was wrong. It never occurred to me to ask one of the regulars. Most experienced lawyers in that courtroom would have been glad to help a novice. I have seldom met a

DOI: 10.4324/9781003533672-5

colleague who would not freely share expertise on how to navigate the system. Other lawyers, court or agency staff members are usually willing to help the newcomer, but help seldom comes if we do not ask.

Practice Good Manners

Treating everyone with respect pays residual dividends – sometimes immediately. Within a few days after my becoming the newest associate in a large law firm, I was sent to the federal court to file a pleading just a few minutes before closing time. I did not know what the pleading was; I had not written it and was not even assigned to the case. My sole task was to get the pleading filed before the clerk's office closed for the day. I approached the high counter and waited until I caught the eye of an assistant clerk. I said, "I'm JB Burtch, a new associate at the firm, and I was told to file this. But I've never filed anything here before and I don't know what to do." The clerk said not to worry. He looked at the papers and said I needed to check this box here, sign on the line there, and otherwise it would be just fine. I did as he instructed, and a great sense of relief washed over me as he pressed the big blue "Filed" stamp onto the document.

As he was finishing up with me, a lawyer from a different firm came through the door, plopped some papers on the counter and said to the clerk, "File these." His tone was abrupt and dismissive. The clerk looked at me and said, "Wait here." It was now about two minutes before closing time. The clerk approached the other lawyer, picked up his papers and examined them silently. He said, "I'm sorry, but these forms aren't filled out right. And we're closing now. You're going to have to take them back to the office, fix them and bring them back tomorrow." That lawyer left, dejected, his unfiled papers in hand. As the door closed, the clerk looked at me and muttered, "Jerk." Lesson learned.

Good manners include dressing the part. If your wardrobe mirrors how your supervisors dress, you send the subtle message that you are preparing to move up. Today, office attire and court attire often differ. Generally, courts expect "business attire," usually meaning suits or coats and ties for men and suits, dresses or slacks and a business top for women. Both differ from "work from home" attire. A trick a friend in the fashion world taught me is "tabletop" dressing, meaning for video meetings, wear professional attire for what shows on the screen and whatever you want for the rest. Dress for the role you are performing, and you will not stand out in the wrong way.

Realize Lawyers Need Clients

The lawyer starting out on her own can have an advantage over the lawyer who works for an established firm. The sole practitioner understands that without a client, she does not have a practice, so she focuses on making herself invaluable to build her practice. Sometimes lawyers joining established practices assume they do not have to develop client relationships because the firm has already done that. That is a short-sighted, career-limiting view. The new big-firm lawyer, even if assigned to an established client, must maintain the relationship going forward. In fact, the stable of solid firm clients is dwindling. Today, sophisticated clients tend to select certain talented lawyers rather than giving all their work to one firm. Law firms still relying on a few large clients run a significant risk. Leadership within organizations changes constantly. Alliances shift. Personal relationships can trump institutional tradition. Clients may switch firms because of dissatisfaction with that firm's performance. But just as often, they switch because they have developed a personal relationship with another lawyer they are confident can do the work just as well or even better.

Client decision makers meet new lawyers all the time. If they meet a new lawyer they trust, they may re-think their legal representation. So, we retain clients if they trust us to handle their work in preference to the other lawyers the clients may know. The lawyer who assumes the client will always be there may have a foreshortened career. Similarly, never assume an organization that would be an attractive client is locked up. Your talent may be the key that opens the door to getting their work.

Discover the Real Problem to Reveal the Solution

Late one afternoon, the administrator of one of my hospital clients called and asked me to come see him as soon as possible. When I arrived at his office, he told me that the director of nursing had fired a nurse because, several nights in a row, she had shown signs of drug impairment.

The administrator summoned me because he had just received a letter from the nurse's lawyer threatening legal action against the hospital. Although normally a flexible person, the administrator was resolute in this matter. He told me he had no intention of settling with the nurse, either for reinstatement or compensation. Using precise legal terms, he said, "JB, when the Supreme Court of the United States turns down our petition for a writ of certiorari, we'll pay." My marching orders were clear.

I knew the lawyer the nurse had retained. Although, like me, he was still relatively new at the bar, he was smart and persistent. I determined the most effective thing I could do was not to keep my client's intentions secret. Unsure of how best to deliver the message, I suggested we meet for a conversation. I invited him to my office, and he accepted.

He arrived at my office with his client, a young, composed woman. The nurse remained in a waiting area while her lawyer and I had our conversation. I wanted to give him a sense of my client's resolve without being condescending or offensive. The power dynamic was already unbalanced, and I feared an aggressive posture on my part would only invite a reciprocal attitude and we would start down a long path with no satisfactory resolution for either party.

I repeated to him, verbatim, what my client had told me. The lawyer listened quietly, without totally disguising his disappointment. He then said, "I'd like you to meet my client. Do you mind if I bring her in?" Of course I agreed, because I did want to meet her and, if possible, hear her story.

When she came in, she told me the charges were false. She said how much they had wounded her pride and, equally important, how humiliated she had felt in front of her family. She said she had felt betrayed by people she trusted. Her theme of humiliation and betrayal came across painfully. She struck me as a straightforward, honest person whose dignity had been offended. I understood why her lawyer had asked me to meet her.

I knew I was in a tight spot. I asked her if I could speak again with her lawyer, alone. The word "dignity" kept running through my mind. When she left, I said to her lawyer, "We need to find a way to restore her dignity so she can put this behind her. No one benefits from a fight over this."

In our meeting she had told me how she had been looking forward to a family gathering in her home that, now, just thinking about it, filled her with shame. I asked her lawyer, "Would it help if, during that family gathering, a florist's truck arrived at her house and she was presented with a huge basket of roses and a note saying something like, 'We're sorry to lose you.'" To his credit, her lawyer didn't reject this thought immediately but said he'd talk it over with her.

I sat in my office for a long time waiting to hear that my idea was rejected. But when her lawyer came back in, he said, "She would appreciate that very much." The next Saturday, the florist's van pulled up in front of her house, and delivered a large basket of roses with an unsigned note. Nothing further transpired. The dispute ended. At the end of the month, I sent the client a bill, but no disbursement for any floral expense was included. The issue here was dignity, not discharge.

The first question a lawyer must ask herself is whether the problem the client presents is, in fact, the real problem for which the client needs resolution. In law school, facts and issues are presented as given. The facts have been determined by a lower court. Real-time life does not work that way. Clients arrive with a problem. Usually, they identify the problem in their own words and tell the lawyer what they want to see happen.

But even before analyzing a problem to sort out any legal issues, the lawyer needs to understand why the client sought legal advice in the first place. Often the problem the client presents is an amalgam of frustrations, emotions, and goals. There may be some legal issue hidden in all this, but the first hurdle is to identify the components of the situation the client presents, test what is real and what is illusory, and then identify the source of energy that propelled the client to bring the situation to a lawyer.

A simple example is when the client arrives with a speeding ticket and a court date. The client asks the lawyer for help in getting the charge either dismissed or reduced. Clear enough. But what if the problem is that one business partner wants to get rid of the other partner he feels contributes little while still taking half the profits? Is the other partner in fact not contributing? Has the business relationship between the partners deteriorated so much that each misperceives the other's motivations?

We cannot always take the client's story at face value. Careful listening – especially for what the client is not saying – is crucial. What the client presents as the problem may be only one symptom of a wider disorder, or something else entirely. But there will be no real solution until the real problem is identified.

Discovering the real issue depends on the lawyer's ability to develop a sufficient relationship of trust, so the client will tell the whole story as fully as possible. The lawyer will be hard-pressed to find any workable solution without first diagnosing the real problem. This requires delving into the real causes of the friction. Only once the real problem is uncovered can the path to a solution emerge.

Just stating the issue in these terms suggests that a lawyer needs to practice psychology without a license. To some extent, that is a fair observation. On the one hand, lawyers are not trained in the process of analyzing human motivation and desire. On the other, without some understanding and insight into why people feel or behave the way they do, the lawyer may miss the root of the problem, misdiagnose it, and embark on a legal strategy that cannot solve it. I have a license that says I am authorized to practice as an "attorney and counsellor at law." The legal counselor part of my license invites me to address problems holistically, including problems driven by human emotion. Here the lawyer's task is, again, to uncover the real problem. Sometimes the lawyer simply needs to bear down on the core dilemma to clarify the real choices involved in reaching a solution.

Suggest a Range of Choices

The legal counseling aspect of the lawyer's role is similarly nuanced. A lawyer must be able to suggest a range of possible choices that are consistent with the client's desires and preferences. The lawyer must listen closely, evaluate potential legal theories (some of which may be inconsistent with each other), and present realistic options so the client can make an autonomous choice, unfettered by the lawyer's own preferences.

There is some controversy about the extent to which the lawyer may advocate his preferred course of action. While restricting options to the client's preferences has been favored in some academic literature,[i] it deprives the client of the lawyer's own expertise. This expertise may have been the very reason the client hired this lawyer in the first place – to get the benefit of his knowledge and experience. Client autonomy does not require a lawyer to stand by idly while the client drives himself off a cliff.

Most people come to a lawyer because they have a problem they cannot solve themselves. The new lawyer will soon see the gap between being trained in legal reasoning and dealing with a person facing an unresolved dilemma. Law students who worked in legal clinics or intern jobs have had a taste of this. But representing a client who is paying a fee for a satisfactory resolution offers a different experience. Clients' expectations may be naïve, but they are real, and they believe they are paying to have those expectations met.

Even the new lawyer has one great advantage the client lacks – a detached perspective. While the lawyer can see the problem from the client's point of view, the lawyer does not share the client's emotional attachments or personal biases. The lawyer's perspective, honed by legal training and insulated by personal detachment, should offer more possible solutions than the client imagined.

Learn to Deliver Bad News Well

Sometimes a lawyer must deliver bad news. There is just no getting around it. The case was dismissed; the motion was denied; the legal theory collapsed. There is no good way to sugarcoat bad news. It needs to be delivered in a straightforward, sympathetic but factual way. Clients need to know where they stand, so their decisions are based in reality.

Early in my career, I watched an accomplished lawyer deal with defeat in a way I have never forgotten. I was working in our small labor library surrounded by piles of case digests, looking for the right line of attack to solve the client issue of the moment. The labor library consisted of one room, one large round table, and a corner table with the only speaker phone on that floor of the firm. The door opened and Mr. Baker, a partner in the firm's litigation section, looked in and said, "Do you mind if we interrupt you and use the speaker phone for a minute?" Of course, I stood up and started to leave as I saw two clients enter with Mr. Baker. "No, don't leave," he said. "We'll just be a minute." So, I sat down and listened. The partner and clients had just returned from a federal court hearing. They had lost a motion, which was a major setback for their case.

The phone call they were making was to the company's president in California. Once he got the president on the phone, the partner was very direct. First, he said in clear, calm terms that they had lost the motion. The president responded that this was bad news and a major loss for the company. Then the partner did something I had not expected. He made no excuses; he did not criticize the judge, the adversary, or anyone else. Rather, he then laid out the three options he thought now were available to the company to move forward. The options presented were specific and clear, given without any suggestion of regret or remorse. The call ended and the three men stood up and left.

But before I went back to the research, I had to process what I had just seen. A firm lawyer returned from a hearing and delivered very unwelcome news to a client. He was calm, organized, and unemotional. He acknowledged the decision was disappointing, but rather than dwelling on feelings and excuses, he moved right on to the plan for moving forward. "Here are the options I see now," he had said, as he proceeded to outline them.

Every case has an emotional component. Lawyers pass the days of their lives crafting arguments and strategies that sometimes fail. Clients pour resources and energy into causes that fail. So, an emotional response to such a setback would not be surprising. The danger, of course, would be to let the emotion dictate the nature of the response.

But that afternoon, Mr. Baker taught me the futility in looking backward with regret. The pertinent topic was, given these new circumstances, what could be done next. Here the lawyer's art was to let the defeat shape the new beginning rather than let it define the matter's end. Loss is inevitable, but defeat is a choice.

Don't Be Afraid to Lead

Clients hire lawyers when they need to effect change but require specialized resources to make that happen. Approaching a problem from a structured, analytical perspective clarifies both mission and execution. New lawyers who feel uncertain about their own leadership ability are often surprised to discover that they do have the clarity of thought essential to cut to the heart of the problem and accomplish the client's goals. Some legal theorists may bristle at the prospect of the lawyer providing strategic leadership, but clients generally expect the lawyer to be part of the team managing the problem. Sometimes they even expect the lawyer to lead the team. It follows naturally that when a client adopts a lawyer's legal strategy to address a problem, the client may rely on the lawyer to carry it through.

A few years ago, I was hired by a company that bought a chain of businesses that was unionized. The employees in each branch were represented by labor unions and my task was to reach new labor contracts with the unions. The company's president said I would be the chief negotiator and, in his words, the "general" of the effort. While, as a lawyer, I was under the direction of my client, the expectation was I was to be the leader in the negotiations. The company's direction to me about its goals was clear. So, it became my job to organize the different teams at each location, gather the data necessary for labor negotiations, and achieve the company's desired results.

Granted, this kind of assignment won't normally come to the new lawyer. Gaining experience, learning to negotiate, using good communication and organization skills, sharpening listening skills, and learning to work with divergent points of view are all essential for the lawyer to become an effective leader. These are the same skills we pick up in the process of becoming better lawyers. Within a firm we learn to lead projects and teams. It is only natural for clients to ask us to take on leadership roles to help achieve their goals. The key is not to avoid leadership, but to step in to it when invited.

Takeaway Tips

Work with purpose
Ask for help
Show respect
Develop client relationships
Define the problem
Offer choices
Learn to deliver bad news well
Take the lead.

Note

i For example, in an early text on client counseling, David Binder and Susan Price (*Legal Interviewing and Counseling: A Client-Centered Approach*, West Group, 1977) stated that "it is our belief that, by and large, lawyers cannot know what value clients really place on the various consequences [of different choices]. We therefore conclude that lawyers usually cannot determine which alternative will provide maximum client satisfaction and that decisions should be left to the client." Id. at 148–149. They add, "It should be stressed that providing the client with the option of choice by the lawyer should usually be the last resort."

CHAPTER V

Conducting Legal Research

Some lawyers, having mastered the art of legal research in law school, shy away from it in practice. Either they do not have access to the same resources they had in school, or they assume that legal research is not as important in their practice as it was in their education. In school, fact patterns tend to be given and fixed; in practice, the facts of a matter constantly evolve as the lawyer interviews more witnesses, reads more documents, or deals with changing client instructions. For whatever reason, the new lawyer needs to understand that the legal landscape may change with each shift in understanding the facts.

This was brought home to me when I was investigating an alleged unfair labor practice case in eastern Kentucky. My client operated coal mines. I had worked with the manager of one of the mines in several previous cases. He was gifted with an almost photographic memory. If he saw it, he remembered it. Early on, I learned that the challenge was to separate pertinent information from the long, detailed stories he recounted.

Earlier in this unfair labor practice dispute, I had interviewed this manager about an accusation that he had threatened to fire some employees who had walked off the job (which, if true, would be an unfair labor practice under the National Labor Relations Act). It was a non-union company, so there was no labor contract prohibiting a strike. The manager said these employees were heading down a hill, away from the mine and toward their cars, when he met them. He told me what he remembered about the incident: "I was walking up the hill and saw some men coming down who should have been working. I got mad and said to the group, 'If you don't get your butts back in that mine right now, I'll find men who will.'" The employees claimed this violated the law because he had threatened them with retaliation for exercising their right to engage in mutual aid and protection by walking out.

I thought the case looked a little grim, because a fact-finder could easily conclude that the men had been threatened with discharge by walking out. Returning to my office the next day, I dug into the law to figure out just how clear-cut a case the employees had and if the manager's words exposed the company to liability. Clearly, employees had a right to engage in "protected concerted activity" and could not be fired for walking off the job. But my

 DOI: 10.4324/9781003533672-6

research uncovered a pleasant surprise. The manager had used exactly the right words. Rather than saying he would "let them go," he said he would "find men who will." The legal research allowed me to conclude he had not threatened to fire or even discipline the employees for walking out. He had simply said he would find men who would do the work, in effect replacing them rather than firing them. Ironically for the employees, the result would be the same: they would lose their jobs (at least until their replacements left). Under the law, the company could not fire or discipline them for leaving the job, but it could replace them for their refusal to work. In this case, legal research led me to the perfect line of cases that helped a client avoid a serious problem.

I showed up at Vanderbilt Law School long before the days of Lexis or Westlaw. Thanks to the patience of my teachers, the law librarian, and some upper-class students, I ultimately got the hang of legal research. Soon, I too began to show some of the obsessive traits of the law student. "What is your authority?" "Is the point holding or dicta?" Even the most obvious assertions could not be made without a citation from a legal source, and everything had to be cited in perfect Bluebook style. I became familiar with the West Key Number system, Shepardizing annotated codes, legal encyclopedias, law reviews, and all kinds of secondary sources. It was not until after I took my first job in a large law firm that I learned the wonders of specialty services such as labor relations reporters, with their exhaustive analytical case digests. It was from reading these case digests that I learned basic labor law. I would sit in our firm's labor library and pore over hundreds of digests looking for just the right holding or language to support a point. Along the way, I picked up all sorts of arcane tidbits. In those days, legal research was like piecing together a jigsaw puzzle to finally reveal the big picture. While this method has become archaic, the challenge of learning a discipline from bits and pieces of cases remains.

Today's legal research is very different. Hours of Shepardizing have been reduced to a few keystrokes. Digital research can be fast and accurate. But no matter what research techniques we are trained to use, finding the law to advance the case is still the lawyer's task. Legal advice provides the client with available alternatives to address a problem, given the constraints of the law. Legal research defines the boundaries and suggests how far the boundaries might be stretched, without breaking, to fit the facts of a case.

Some lawyers fall into a subtle trap in the transition from law school to law practice. Their training in structured thinking and their confidence in intuitive solutions may short-circuit the impulse to dig deep into the law. Common sense is indispensable once the parameters of the legal issues have been defined, but common sense is no substitute for legal research. Presented with any situation where a client seeks advice, the new lawyer must assume that (1) there are legal principles governing the situation, (2) these principles may not be readily apparent, and (3) legal research will be necessary to illuminate the whole picture.

Generally, clients are not interested in legal developments, theories, or nuances. Clients want their problems solved. This marks the fault line between academic lawyers (law professors and legal commentators) and practicing lawyers (lawyers who represent clients). Some lawyers have a foot in both camps, but they are the exception. Academic lawyers research for ideas and theory; practicing lawyers research for the client. Legal research is the foundation of both.

Read the File

One of the advantages of hiring new lawyers right out of law school is their familiarity with the latest techniques in legal research. But it is the gap between the posited facts of law school exercises and the mutable facts of client problems that can confuse the new lawyer. In client situations, facts are more fluid than case hypotheticals. After the lawyer reads the file, she may realize there are competing or inconsistent versions of the facts in a case. With subsequent interviews or investigation, new facts may emerge, and situations once accepted as given become ambiguous. This does not assume mendacity; it assumes ordinary human fallibility and the uncertain availability of helpful documents. That is why the first thing a lawyer should do after being assigned a case is read the file. It gives the big picture, suggests the nature of the problem, and discloses areas for further exploration. Legal research is best postponed until the lawyer has absorbed the file and has a better sense of what needs further investigation.

Useful legal research identifies those paths that are available, unavailable, and those, if the facts were different, could become available. The goal is to identify those legal theories that are most likely to reach the client's goals, and to identify the facts in the case that support the theory. If there is a statute that may govern the matter, review the statute. If theories emerge from the file, dig in to the facts that support each available theory. They will provide the road map to fully develop the legal underpinnings of the case. The place to start is to read the file and see what facts are already established and those that need to be further developed.

Consult Experienced Lawyers

Experienced lawyers can also be of great help. When I received my first research assignment from a partner, he told me to begin my work by looking at the terms "appropriate bargaining unit" and "community of interest." These, he said, were likely to be found in the cases that would point me toward the answers to the key questions. He was telling me the legal terms he would explore were he researching the project. Even if these words weren't perfectly on point, they were closer than any place I would have begun on my own.

A brief conversation with a lawyer who has been down this road before can save hours of research. Not all supervisors are equally helpful, but asking other lawyers in the firm where they would start is both flattering and effective.

Search Secondary Resources

Secondary resources are the legal encyclopedias, treatises, law review articles, and specialty services (all now online) that give the big picture of the area being researched. They introduce the framework of the law, the key concepts, and seminal cases that provide the jumping-off point for more specific inquiry. The problem with moving directly to the case or statute databases is they pull up too much information that may be irrelevant to the issue at hand. Starting with cases or statutes takes more time than beginning research using a secondary resource. Once the useful threads are found, it is time to dive into the databases. Consider whether Boolean or more natural search terms work best. Artificial intelligence has made natural language searches more productive, but Boolean, used well, often pulls up more on-point cases quicker. (This may become less true as artificial intelligence improves natural language searches.)

Not surprisingly, legal blogs or law firm websites often provide helpful overviews of specific subjects. Beginning the research process with a general web search can be both dangerous and productive. It is dangerous because it offers so many false starts and paths of misinformation. Experienced lawyers can use Google searches more safely because they know the map of dead ends. Newer lawyers need to be cautious using general web searches. But they can also turn up productive leads to better information.

After finding some helpful cases (even those that hold differently from the desired result), you should narrow the search to find where a holding is directly on point or where the analysis leads directly to a desired outcome. Having now found a circle of authority and some pertinent quotes to bring it all home, check each case again to ascertain if it is still current law. Even if it is flagged as disfavored, the point may be so well stated that it is still worth citing, so long as you note its disfavored status. Now, armed with good law, the lawyer can write the brief, make the argument, or advise the client.

Not all new lawyers have access to online proprietary research services. And when they do, they need to pay attention to whether their search falls within their firm's service subscription plan. Searching beyond the firm's plan can rack up costs that an associate may find hard to explain. Some bar associations provide online legal research services as part of their membership benefits. University or bar association law libraries may offer lawyers free access to some databases. Most federal and state laws and regulations are free online through government websites. The good news for new lawyers is that legal sources are becoming more open rather than more restrictive, and the cost of legal research continues to decline.

Know When to Stop

Once when I was a fledgling lawyer, I showed a draft of a bill to one of the firm's senior partners. The draft itemized the work we had done for the client, including my noting "thorough legal research" on a particular point. The partner scrutinized the draft carefully, then pulled out his large, black fountain pen and scratched through one word in my draft. He asked me to step around his desk so I could see the change. He had scratched through the word "thorough." Nervously, I asked why he made the change. Much of that bill represented my legal research, which was as thorough as I could make it. His eyes were twinkling behind his clear, round glasses as he replied, "Mr. Burtch, all the legal research we do here is thorough."

But even thorough research has an end point. Your goal is to find the answers that help make the case. There needs to be a clear path, not a paved highway. While endless research may be pleasurable for the curious lawyer, its marginal productivity may strain both the client's budget and patience. Good legal research is exhaustive without being encyclopedic. Clients want answers, not treatises.

Master a Specialty

Once the lawyer's research has developed her expertise in an area of the law and it becomes an important part of her practice, it is time to master that area. Gain expertise by attending continuing legal education conferences or presentations that offer an overview of the latest developments. It only makes sense to build up the store of knowledge in your area of concentration. If your state has a mandatory CLE requirement for lawyers, it is wise to seek out programs consistent with your practice rather than just stacking up credits.

One of my more embarrassing memories is driving for hours to attend a day-and-a-half conference on drafting wills and powers of attorney – legal work I have seldom touched. The conference was scheduled one week before the CLE deadline, and I needed the credits to keep my license current. The hotel ballroom was packed with lawyers like me, lawyers whose practices did not involve estate planning. But also, like me, they were facing the CLE deadline. Advanced planning would have helped us all save a wasted two days.

One effective way to master an area of law is to write about it. New cases provide the opportunity to write explanations about why the cases are significant in your area of the law. These can be offered to bar association journals or even posted on your firm's website. They are usually noticed twice: first, when they are published, and second, when they pop up in a web search for a particular topic. Thus, the process of writing about the law, which necessarily requires learning it, benefits both author and reader. The author becomes known for expertise in the area, and the reader benefits from learning about it.

Takeaway Tips

Read the file
Consult experienced lawyers
Search secondary resources
Know when to stop
Master a specialty.

CHAPTER VI

Practicing in a Firm

Usually, the new lawyer begins his or her career practicing as an associate lawyer in an established law firm. Within law firms there is usually a division between litigation and transactional work. In law school, especially early on, the curriculum concentrates on the litigation side. Foundational legal concepts are taught through the analysis of cases: how courts determine the facts of a dispute, what legal principles apply, and what outcome flows from the application of facts to legal principles. Litigation practice, thus, centers on disputes and their resolution. Litigators investigate the origins of the dispute, research what legal theories may apply, find evidence to support the theories of recovery or defense, and determine what witnesses and documents should be brought before a tribunal to best persuade it in favor of their desired outcome. Litigators should be comfortable with conflict, skilled in negotiation, and have a sense of knowing what arguments will be the most persuasive. They need to be adept at organizing facts and data while, at the same time, being agile in handling a client's changing desires and goals.

Transactional lawyers make deals. They form and restructure businesses, handle mergers, arrange acquisitions, and negotiate business financing arrangements. They draft documents, write estate plans, make due diligence investigations, all with an eye to avoiding the disputes that lead to litigation. Transactional lawyers tend to be analytical and detail oriented. They understand business and enjoy crafting solutions to complex business problems. Fundamentally, litigators are concerned with attacking or defending past events, while transactional lawyers focus on shaping the future. To oversimplify, litigators and transactional lawyers work by looking in opposite directions.

Few students decide to enter solo practice directly from law school. Usually, that is a decision made after a lawyer has achieved a comfortable level of experience and decides that practicing alone better suits them. But there are times, such as economic recession, when setting out on one's own may be the only viable choice. Some former obstacles to solo practice have been reduced or eliminated. Access to legal information, through web research, legal databases, and low-cost legal search engines are now more available to

 DOI: 10.4324/9781003533672-7

the solo practitioner. The challenge remains how to ensure that the information received is both accurate and current. But any lawyer carrying a smartphone has a pocket library that prior generations could only dream of.

The three biggest challenges facing the new solo are gaining professional competence, learning to run a business, and obtaining clients. Checklists on how to set up a solo firm are available on many bar association websites. This could include registering the practice with a state bar, setting up operating and trust accounts, obtaining malpractice insurance, and keeping current with continuing education requirements. Just asking experienced solo practitioners how they set up their firm and developed competence is a good place to start. Talking with these lawyers offers insight into the challenges and opportunities of solo practice. While some may balk at sharing their knowledge, others will welcome it and share generously. Most established lawyers enjoy telling new ones how they pulled it all together.

Building a client base is more difficult. Court clerks and judges can advise the new lawyer on how to become eligible to get on court-appointed lists. While the compensation is less than representing private clients, the connections gained can lead to attracting those private clients. So, the most important thing for the new solo is to build a network that can refer cases. Take every opportunity to meet other lawyers and participate in bar activities. The more lawyers are in your network, the more opportunities there are to be referred cases. Let every family member and friend know what you are trying to achieve and the kind of work you seek. Often, lawyers get referrals from people they have only met casually. Even friends of friends may call for help if they heard you could handle their problem. Bar association newsletters need articles. Writing a short article on a new legal development can make the author stand out as a lawyer to be sought out. Publishing establishes reputation and builds brand. Not all lawyers are suited for solo practice, but for those who are, the rewards are enormous.

Whether you are working in a large or small firm or as a solo practitioner, learn these principles sooner rather than later to avoid heartburn.

Understand the Assignment

When you are given an assignment, do not begin working without knowing (1) exactly what you are supposed to do and (2) how the assignor (supervisor or client) envisions the final product. For example, the supervising lawyer may say, "I need some help in the Jones matter. I can't remember if Virginia is a 7-year or a 21-year state for adverse possession. Can you take care of this?"

Sounds simple, doesn't it? Just do some legal research and find out your state's rules for adverse possession. But does the supervisor want a written memo? If so, will a short, conclusive answer suffice, or do they expect a detailed analysis of adverse possession? Will an oral report do? Are you supposed to figure out how the adverse possession issue fits into the larger issues in the Jones matter, or is this simply a one-shot inquiry? Have you just been assigned to the Jones case, or are you only performing a limited research project? The assigning lawyer may not be clear about what she wants, even in her own mind. You are not a mind reader, so you will not understand the scope of the assignment unless you ask. Your question may prompt the assignor to think through what she really needs from you. If you neglect to ask, there is a good possibility that whatever you produce will not meet her expectations. Sometimes the associate must make the partner clarify the scope of an assignment, or else the associate risks disappointing the partner's undefined expectations.

Many associates are intimidated by a partner's seemingly preoccupied or distracted manner. Partners are busy and associates want to be useful but are afraid to take up too much of the busy partner's time. Yet if your understanding and the partner's expectations are different, it will take much longer to get the assignment done right. Knowing exactly what is expected at the outset enhances associate success and results in the most efficient approach.

The same principles apply if a client assigns a project. If you are the only lawyer dealing with the client, use the same approach you would with an assigning partner. But also consider how the scope of the task may affect the overall budget for the project. Once the client understands the economic effect of the request, he may narrow or even withdraw the assignment if the cost is disproportionate to the benefit.

I had to learn this the hard way. I once had a client who was a master of the "what if." I understood he wanted advice on the risks involved in making a specific offer and thought we had an agreed-upon approach. But then, I would get a phone call: "What if we decided to add an indemnification clause to our offer? Would that make a difference?" There would then follow three or four other "what ifs," all changing the assumptions of the original query. Shortly after we decided to go with the original offer, I sent a bill for that month's work. Then I got a call from the client saying my bill was about three times what he was expecting. I thought his "what ifs" were questions he wanted answered to help him reformulate the offer. But as it turned out, asking these "what if" questions was just the way he liked to ponder options in his own mind. They were not questions he expected me to research, although, in fairness to me, they needed legal analysis or even research before I responded to them. Ultimately, we did develop a strong working relationship, but only after I understood his way of thinking.

Read the File

This point bears repeating. It may seem obvious, but it is a step that is too often overlooked by new lawyers. Legal questions from clients never arise in the abstract. The file tells you what the case is about, what the client wants, how the problem arose, and what other lawyers may or may not know about the matter. By reading the file, you get an overview of the case – which may differ from what you have been told. Reading the file before you begin a memo results in your turning in a more complete and useful piece of work. It is not hard to spot work produced by an associate who has failed to absorb information in the file. Assumptions and abstractions proliferate, and the specific facts get short shrift. The associate who begins by reading the file becomes a useful associate on the case, and if you become useful on enough cases, you will achieve the closest thing this profession offers to job security.

Learn the Jargon

The lingo of any specialty is confusing at first. Other lawyers speak as if you know what they are saying. It takes time to understand, so pay attention and soak it up. If words or phrases that you do not yet know are part of an assignment, look them up or ask what they mean. Or just nod and listen for context. The lawyer who is talking to you has probably forgotten how clueless she was in her first months out of law school. Just pay attention, and it won't be long until you are slinging around legal jargon just like everyone else.

Focus on the Outcome

A Richmond federal judge gave a speech I've never forgotten. He was a man who loved to hunt. Lawyers, he said, get distracted by peripheral issues in cases. His solution to distraction was to "keep your eye on the rabbit." By this he meant that every case has a desired outcome (getting the rabbit). If your efforts are not being directed toward the desired outcome, you are wasting your time.

Some new lawyers become unduly fascinated by the many issues presented in even a simple case. They see innumerable opportunities, so they research every possible angle to undermine an adversary's claims before solidifying their own client's case. If there are documents or witness interviews that will make the client's version unassailable, the lawyer needs to make sure they are solid before going down other paths. In most situations, only a few critical points move a case forward. Focus on these. Keeping your eye on the rabbit shows that you know what is important. Some lawyers confuse activity with achievement. Activity may run up a bill but, without focus, it does not improve the case. Staying busy is not the goal; achieving the goal is.

Speak Deliberately

Our profession has a long and colorful oral tradition. Before the introduction of the printing press – probably even before handwriting – advocates were advancing causes using only their power of speech. Even now that digital communication prevails, lawyers use speech to persuade tribunals and juries. But the power of speech in the office is sometimes overlooked.

It is important for the new lawyer to speak deliberately and with purpose. Casual, informal conversations are certainly appropriate in the office when not discussing work. Conversations with supervisors and other lawyers about current cases, however, are professional discourse. Their purpose is to ask something, explain something, or offer an opinion or comment on a matter. As such, they need to be thought through and delivered with precision. This may not be as challenging as it sounds. It is not unlike responding to a professor's questions in class. You are prepared, know the issues, and can explain what facts affect the result. Speaking deliberately in the office displays the new lawyer's understanding that the building blocks of legal advice are formed from the orderly, analytical explanation of the case's determinative issues. The dialogue between lawyers tests the validity and persuasiveness of the arguments until they become advice offered to the client or points made before a tribunal.

More introverted lawyers may fear the silences that occur as they form their thoughts. It is the thought, not the silence, that matters. Conversely, more extroverted lawyers may fear that by appearing to think out loud – offering contradictory or inconsistent statements on the same point – they undercut their effectiveness. To eliminate this, all the extroverted lawyer need do is interject something like, "I'm thinking with my mouth right now; bear with me and we'll get it right." In either case, new lawyers can demonstrate an understanding that oral expression, even in the office, is a professional skill they are on the way to mastering.

Asking questions is one of the fundamental skills of our craft. But before you ask a supervisor a question, be sure you have done everything to find the answer yourself. If the answer to the question is in the file, why haven't you read the file? If the answer is in a book or legal resource, why didn't you look there first? Your supervisor assumes you have read the file and done some preliminary research. Doing this preliminary work sharpens your questions.

When you ask a question, formulate it before you speak. That shows you understand the problem even if you do not know the answer. Ask the most important question first. That shows you understand priorities. When answering a question, be honest and clear. If you do not know the answer, say so. Smart partners and clients are good smoke detectors. No one likes to be fed a line, especially not clients who are paying for your help. If you do not know an answer, estimate the time and research it will take to get the answer. Then proceed to follow the schedule you promised.

Avoid starting your answer with "it depends." Of course, the answer depends on many factors, and you should lay them out clearly. But starting the answer with "it depends" raises red flags. First, it is the archetypical lawyer answer.

Second, it suggests you have not completely thought the question through or might prefer to avoid it altogether. New lawyers can become embarrassed by not knowing all the answers, so they tend to temporize rather than display the limitations of their knowledge. Just give the best answer you can and assure the questioner you will follow up.

Avoid Shortcuts

You do not yet know enough about the law or the problem presented to take shortcuts. It is that simple. When you are thoroughly familiar with an area of the law and equally familiar with the type of challenge before you, you might employ some shortcuts. Until then, avoid them. They lead to dead ends. Lawyers who prematurely adopt shortcuts usually must start all over from the beginning and do it again, the right way.

Delegate With Care

Few things irritate a supervisor more than having an assignment boomerang. Suppose I am the assigning attorney, and I ask an associate to research something like the simple adverse possession question. The associate may think this question is somewhat beneath her because it involves looking up an answer that should be easy to find. She may be wondering why I did not do it myself or give it to my experienced legal assistant. So, the associate discusses the question with the legal assistant. The legal assistant says he will find out. But he is busy with other tasks or thinks this request is too much trouble for him to go through to help a new associate. So, the legal assistant, somewhat annoyed at the associate, walks into my office and poses the question back to me: the very same question I asked the associate to research. What has happened is that the associate has just reassigned the problem to me – adding to my workload rather than helping to reduce it.

The reason we have office assistants, law clerks and legal assistants is to pass down work to the least expensive employee who can perform that job competently. What the lawyer must do herself and what she can delegate requires some judgement. Obviously, preparation of an exhibit book for trial can be delegated to a legal assistant. But the lawyer must supervise the project because, ultimately, it is the lawyer's responsibility.

Communicate

Keep the partner or the client up to date on your progress. Copy them on all significant correspondence. Clients and supervisors should not have to ask about the status of a matter. They should already be in the loop. Return client phone calls the same day to avoid creating an unhappy client.

Learn to Operate Office Equipment

My father was not a lawyer, but he gave me some important practical advice. Dad was president of a small manufacturing plant in Ohio. His own father had been an estate caretaker and boatbuilder on the St. Lawrence River. Dad grew up knowing how to use machinery – though as company president, that skill was not in his job description. One day he was walking through the plant, dressed in his usual blue suit, when a machine operator stopped him and said, "Jack, I can't get this saw to cut the new steel. We need to get a different saw if we are going to use this kind of steel." Dad said nothing. He just took off his suit jacket, walked over to the machine, made a few adjustments, and started cutting the steel rods to the required length. In retelling this story, he said to me, "JB, it's a lot easier to run a plant if you know how everything works."

After I took my first job as a new lawyer, I ended up working a lot of holidays and weekends. No staff was around, but the copying machines still broke down. So, I learned how to change the ink cartridges, load reams of paper, and fix the inevitable jams. Every lawyer needs to know how to complete work, either in hard copy or digitally. This means the lawyer must have at least elementary competence in operating the office's essential hardware and software. The lawyer who cannot operate every office machine and use every program becomes a hostage to the staff. The lawyer may well be working after the staff has gone home. In short, there is no process necessary to get work completed that a lawyer should not be able to do.

Learn Filing Procedures

Most new lawyers think that once the draft of the brief is finished, they are close to the finish line. After it has been edited and dropped into the prescribed format, it will be ready to go. This is magical thinking.

Once you believe you have completed the draft, your supervising attorney will want to review it. She may have criticisms, suggestions, new ideas, or even a completely different approach. Giving the supervisor ongoing progress reports on a brief may preclude her wanting it totally rewritten at the last minute. Keep your supervisor in the loop and incorporate suggested changes so the draft can be reviewed again. Even when the brief is accepted by your team as final, it is still not ready to file.

If you do not already know, you will need to understand the court's requirements for how the brief should be formatted and presented. Are there page limits, font requirements, or the need for a table of cases? How many copies does the court want? Even with electronic filing, some judges still want their own paper copy of a pleading. Are you supposed to send a hard copy to a clerk's office or judge's chambers? Most of this information will be in the court's local rules, but some will not. Different judges in the same district often have different preferences about filings. If you are new to a court, visit the clerk's office and ask an assistant clerk to introduce you to the ground rules. There may even be local rules for that court. You will learn current practice while beginning to develop a working relationship with the clerk's office. If you accomplish that, your future encounters will be smoother.

The process of shepherding a draft from final form to "Filed" differs from court to court. The easiest way to avoid the stress of a last-minute filing is to know in advance the requirements for filing. My own rule of thumb is to allow almost as much time to get the papers ready to file as it took to get a good draft finished.

Finish the Job

Your supervising lawyer is neither your research assistant nor your editor. Few things frustrate a partner more than having a lawyer turn in a draft of a document that has not been completely researched, analyzed, and finished by the associate. It is irritating for a partner to receive an email from an associate enclosing a "rough draft" of the assignment she was given. Maybe the associate was insecure about her work and titled it "rough draft" to cover herself. To a partner, "rough draft" means the associate has failed to finish the job. If you are uncertain about how far to take an analysis or whether every possible issue should be thoroughly developed, ask the partner for direction before submitting a draft. If you turn in a completed piece of work – the best you can do – the partner may edit and revise it, or not. But, if the partner feels she must finish it herself because the work you did was incomplete, she will resent it. Returning the assignment completed and in the expected format enhances your reputation as a valuable team member.

When I neglected to turn in a project completed and on time, an understanding partner gave me a lesson I've never forgotten. I was sitting at my desk when Mark, a corporate partner outside my section, stopped in the doorway and asked if he could speak to me for a minute. He came in, closed the door, and sat down. I knew why he was there; shame and fear ran through me. Several weeks earlier he'd asked me to write a memo about an employment issue facing one of his clients. He'd said there was no rush. Normally that meant he should get it in about ten days, but I had done nothing, and ten days were long past. I had my list of excuses ready, but as I was preparing to mount my defense, he said something totally unexpected.

"JB, every lawyer has a project they just can't start or just can't finish. That has happened to me more than once and it's always embarrassing. I don't want you to dig yourself into the same hole I've been in. I hear you're going out of town next week for that coal project. You'll have plenty of time alone in a motel room to get this done. Just sit down and do it and I'll look for the memo shortly after you return." He got up, thanked me for my time and left.

The first thing I did when I got to the motel the next day was to start on the memo. Client meetings took up the next few days, but the evenings I devoted to the memo. By the time I got back, it was in pretty good shape. I polished it up and handed Mark the memo the next day. All he said was, "Thanks, JB. You feel a lot better now, don't you?" Yes, I was hugely relieved. What had started as a small project had taken on a life of its own. Every day I failed to address the project, it became more menacing. I hadn't wanted to think about it. It loomed like a dark cloud over everything else I was doing. My procrastination made the project seem far more difficult than it turned out to be.

I have never forgotten this encounter. What struck me was Mark's graciousness when he came into my office. There were no accusations or recriminations. There was just a dose of reality followed by his personally identifying with the problem. In the years since then, I've tried to adopt Mark's approach when I'm faced with an associate stuck on an assignment. Some supervisors use fear as a motivator, but long-term, that eats away at the work relationship and breeds cynicism. Encouragement inspires good performance. Today when I'm stuck, I remember Mark and just sit down to do it.

Watch Your Hours

Most firms still track an associate's hours, whether they are part of the billing agreement with the client or not. Many firms also have hour expectations for associates. If you are putting in the kind of effort it takes to succeed, these should not be a problem. There is also the expectation that associates will devote time to pro bono cases that serve clients unable to pay legal fees. Some firms also record nonbillable time for firm tasks such as administrative duties and writing projects. The partners, however, tend to focus on billable hours. Whatever the firm says about its devotion to public service, billable hours remain the bottom line. Pay attention to yours.

Takeaway Tips

Understand the assignment
Read the file
Learn the jargon
Focus on the outcome
Speak deliberately
Avoid shortcuts
Delegate with care
Communicate
Learn to use office equipment
Learn filing procedures
Finish the job
Watch your hours.

CHAPTER VII

Handling a Case

A prominent federal judge once gave a talk to the Virginia Bar Association about what a lawyer should do when a new case arrives in the office. "The first thing a lawyer should do," he said, "is close the door to the office, silence the phone, sit back and just think about the case. Do nothing else. Take some time and think about the case."

This is precisely the opposite of what often happens. A new matter arrives, and the lawyer starts plotting moves even before the case, complaint, or demand letter has been thoroughly analyzed. This approach is fueled by adrenaline rather than logic. Activity eclipses strategy. The inherent risk of this approach is the strategic die may be cast before the most creative approach can even be considered. Of course, the new lawyer is seldom the lead in a case and may be given instructions with the expectation that things happen immediately. But this does not overrule the admonition to first close the door and think about the case.

Ponder the Case

Lawsuits reflect unresolved conflicts. One side thought starting a court process was the next right step toward a favorable result. This doesn't mean that party intended to see the court process through to the end; it just means they saw filing suit as the best alternative to achieve their goal. Some courts make withdrawing a suit difficult. Plaintiffs who haven't thought the process through can find themselves locked in litigation longer than they intended. While a lawsuit is seldom the most effective way to resolve a dispute, it may be the only available way to open a meaningful conversation with a stubborn adversary. Well over 90% of all lawsuits are settled prior to a court decision, and many more disputes are settled prior to filing a suit. Litigation, however, is probably the most expensive form of conversation imaginable.

The new lawyer will be guided by the supervisor in what steps to take when a new case arrives. Different supervisors will have different approaches and styles and the new lawyer can learn from them all. But even though the new lawyer will be acting under the direction of a supervisor, he will be

DOI: 10.4324/9781003533672-8

well served to keep in mind how he would propose to handle the matter if it were left up to him. Unless he thinks it through on his own, engages his own analytical process of deciding the best strategy and the best next tactical moves, he will not appreciate fully the rationale behind the supervisor's instructions. Even though the new lawyer's role in a case may be limited, the lawyer's thought process is not. It is worth thinking about alternatives to the chosen tribunal. If the case were brought in state court, are there advantages to removing it to federal court if it could have jurisdiction? Would arbitration be a better forum for all parties? Is there an opportunity to mediate the dispute? The point is that the new lawyer learns how to handle a case by thinking about all the forces that formed the dispute and all the available alternatives for resolution.

Keep it simple. If you break the case down into its component parts, strategies may present themselves that may otherwise have been overlooked. Preparation is both easier and more effective, even in a complex matter, when issues are addressed one at a time. For the new lawyer, this can make a complicated case less overwhelming.

Early in my own career, I received clear guidance from my boss about my role as the most junior lawyer in case decisions. He said, "You can present any ideas you think are right and you can argue for them all you want. But after I decide what advice we are giving the client, your job is to go along with the plan." I thought this was a fair – even generous – balance between respecting my contribution as a lawyer and my role as a team member.

Part of being a team player is knowing how much contact, if any, a supervising lawyer wants a junior lawyer to have with a client. Some lawyers can be very controlling about the extent an associate is permitted to communicate with the client. Some lawyers assert a claim of ownership of the client, so that any contact that does not include them is seen as an intrusion on their exclusive relationship.

In law school, I clerked for a small insurance defense law firm defending against claims of trailer park residents after a tornado had ripped through their neighborhood. My boss was out of town, and I had a question about one of the files. So, I phoned the insurance company's contact in Chicago who gladly gave me the answer and seemed pleased we were so far along on the matter. Upon return, my boss was not pleased at all. He was angry that I had interfered with his client relationship. My initiative was taken as interference. I have never agreed with his reaction, but I have also never forgotten it.

Think again about how the parties came into conflict in the first place. At every point, the right question to ask is, "What is the real issue here?" While this question may seem beyond the role of the junior lawyer, it is essential to ask even if the new lawyer is expected to keep her thoughts to herself. The assigning lawyer may be caught up in distractions and details and not even considering these larger issues. If the junior lawyer keeps an eye on the bigger picture, she will understand her assignments more completely and may be able to offer an additional perspective on how the matter can be handled.

The new lawyer should get in the habit of exploring how a dispute arose, who the interested parties are, whether there are disparities of interest within different factions, and what the ultimate goals of each party or faction are. In so doing, she gains insights that become important as the dispute develops through the process of litigation to the process of resolution.

When a case comes in, there is a response to be made, witnesses to be consulted, discovery to be planned, and hours to be billed. Some lawyers equate a client's sending a case with an invitation to commence no-holds-barred litigation. Especially if feelings are running high, some clients love to know their lawyer is ready to return to the other side a full measure of the same hostility they received. Sometimes this approach is the right one, but often the wiser course is to consider the alternatives before committing to a litigation process.

Ultimately, the challenge is to discern the client's real objective. Is it to win this case or solve a problem? For the client, litigation is an emotional process. The stated objective at the outset may not be the real objective at the end. A client's desires can change several times during the process of trial preparation. Part of the lawyer's job is to discern clients' shifting attitudes while encouraging them to keep their sights on the real problem.

Once a dispute has progressed beyond its initial stage, the recurring fees and expenses may cause the client to reconsider whether litigation is achieving the goal or worth the cost. What the client once held as a matter of principle can transform into a stalemate and expense the client resents. When a lawyer brings up settlement ideas in the initial discussion with the client, the lawyer may be criticized as being insufficiently aggressive. Later, the very same lawyer may be criticized for not getting the case settled earlier, before costs became oppressive.

When a case first arrives in the office, the lawyer responsible needs to discover what outcome the client desires and communicate this to all other lawyers working on the matter. But sometimes lawyers just make assumptions about what clients want and start out thinking in the wrong direction. Begin by learning how the problem arose and what the client wants to see happen. If the client is an organization, who makes the decisions and what are the different interests within the organization that will affect those decisions? If the client is an important firm client, the new lawyer should consider how the law firm's own interests may introduce a subtle bias into the decision process. Is the client under new management, so the firm wants to prove itself to the new team? Is the client slow to pay, so the firm needs to protect itself financially? Even though lawyers have clear ethical duties to act in the best interests of the client, it is naive to think a firm has no independent interests that may affect its advice. Continuing to pose the question "what is really going on here?" forces the new lawyer to keep the client's best interests at the forefront of any decision. It reminds the lawyer that legal creativity is an essential part of law practice.

Creativity is lost when case handling becomes rote. Lawyers trust the usual approach because it usually produces good results. But that's not a good reason to adopt it without thinking it through. In some kinds of practices, cases are routine. A defense firm that handles negligence suits has templates for answers, motions, and discovery. But every case deserves its own legal analysis. There may be just one fact or circumstance that raises a different legal issue or opens the door to a different approach. Part of the joy of being a lawyer is finding that slight differences of fact or theory have significant legal consequences. Lawyers who limit their practice to one area sometimes become jaded and do not expect to find anything new. Here the new lawyer can take advantage of her own inexperience by seeking out any legal theory that may fit the facts. There will be plenty of dead ends, but there also may be a breakthrough. If nothing else, the effort will make the new lawyer a master of the law on the case.

Prove the Legal Theory

The legal theory is the plaintiff's case road map. It determines the elements that must be proven for the theory to succeed. If the common law definition of burglary is "the breaking and entering of the dwelling place of another in the nighttime with the intent to commit a felony," then there must be facts to support each element, or else burglary cannot be proven. Some other crime may stick, but not burglary. Thus, the legal theory defines the evidence needed to make the case. The legal theory is also the defendant's road map. To undermine the theory of burglary, a defendant's task is to knock out one of the definitional elements of the theory. If the event happened during daylight, it's not burglary. Removing any one element destroys that one theory. Keeping the legal theories firmly in mind promotes efficient and creative handling of the case.

Size Up the Opposition

Our adversarial system requires that lawyers think about the case from the perspective of the opposing side. What does the adversary really want? What is the adversary's back story? How is the adversary's law firm connected with its client? All the considerations that presented themselves on the client's side of the case apply to the other side as well. Find out about the lawyers on the other side. Check their available public information, their websites, and social media. Query mutual acquaintances. Gathering information about the adversary's lawyers may offer a sneak peek at how they handle cases, their temperaments, and their negotiation styles. Analyzing the opposing interests gives the new lawyer a clearer picture of the whole case. It will not be totally accurate, because there is no way to guarantee accurate perception with limited knowledge. But the habit of looking for these answers will produce a better strategy.

One of the advantages of practicing in a cohesive legal community is building relationships of trust with other lawyers. It is far easier to try a case against counsel you trust than against counsel you don't know or don't trust. When opposing counsel demonstrates bad behavior, confront it. Protect yourself from unwarranted accusations by documenting conversations with opposing counsel and sending them emails or letters outlining what has been agreed or discussed. Admittedly, these all take time. But in the long run they are worth it to avoid the consequences of opposing counsels' reneging on their word.

Early in my career, I was handed a small matter that was scheduled for trial in a few weeks. I didn't know plaintiff's counsel, so I asked one of the senior members of our firm what he would be like as an opponent. The partner said, "Your case is never going to trial. That guy hasn't tried a case in thirty years." I was surprised to discover there are lawyers like that. Being unwilling to try a case leads to settling on less favorable terms. So, I kept my settlement offers very low, knowing that if he would never try the case, it would be a mistake to let any offer get into his settlement range until the very last minute when the pressure of time worked to my client's advantage.

Studying the power relationship between the parties illuminates hidden parameters of the dispute. Power is always a factor, though not always obvious. Weaker parties may seem intransigent because they do not want to feel pushed. Stronger parties may contest every point just to stress the adversary's finances. Analyzing these dynamics removes some of the mystery from relationships, allowing a clearer view of the real opportunities.

Investigate the Judge

It is just as important to find out about the judge. Most lawyers will share freely their experience with judges. Knowing whether a judge is fair but firm, easygoing and casual, or unpredictably prickly can make a big difference in how a case gets presented. Once I was going against lawyers for a federal agency who failed to appreciate one federal judge's mercurial personality. Even experienced lawyers found chambers conferences with this judge to be an anxiety-provoking ordeal. The agency had overlooked the time deadlines in the judge's pretrial order, assuming they would get more time if they asked for it. At the final pretrial conference, they arrived unprepared and received a blistering rebuke. The next day, the agency sent a Stipulation of Dismissal, thus ending the case. The agency had decided at the last minute that its only option was to fold its tent and move on. A few preliminary phone calls to local lawyers to learn more about this judge might have saved their case.

Tailor Discovery

The best place to begin a discovery plan is with the client. Usually, the client already knows much of the information the other side has. Broad "fishing expedition" discovery, normal in the past, may be sanctionable today. It is easy to spend a client's money by making broad discovery requests (which will be opposed by objection), then narrowing the scope with opposing counsel and finally asking a court to compel production of the important information that remains undisclosed. Since some courts assess fees against the losing side of a discovery dispute, a motion to compel must be tailored to produce key facts or it should not be filed. Otherwise, the process is even more expensive and risks producing nothing of real value, or even worse, producing a sanction.

One approach is to consider each element of each legal theory presented and then draft discovery requests pertinent to establishing or undermining each element. For the new lawyer, using a form to draft discovery may be a useful way to start the process. Forms can be both safety nets and confidence builders. But a form is only a starting point. Each question must be crafted to uncover information that moves this case forward.

Prepare Witnesses

As a young lawyer, I found myself thrust into some situations I had to figure out for myself. In the first arbitration I handled, as second chair, my boss called from out of town to ask if I had the witnesses prepared. "Of course," I answered. I had contacted each of them, told them the time and place of the hearing, and made sure their schedules were clear. "Did you talk with them about what they are going to say in their testimony?" my boss responded. That never occurred to me. The truth is, until that moment, I didn't know what "preparing a witness" meant.

We discuss the witness's testimony with them for many reasons. We want to be sure that what they have to say supports our case or undermines the adversary's. We go over testimony to be sure the story is compact, comprehensible, and truthful, so a fact-finder will be more likely to see things our client's way. Similarly, we prepare witnesses for cross-examination by making sure they give only the shortest truthful answer to any question. Obviously, the answer must be truthful. But it also needs to be short. Narrative responses only give the cross-examiner more opportunity to ask more questions. We remind the witness not to accept any invitation by opposing counsel to speculate or affirm opposing counsel's assumptions. We want to be sure their testimony will be accurate, believable, and effective.

Truth is the non-negotiable element of any witness's testimony. If a witness cannot or will not tell the truth, we cannot call them to testify. The first thing I tell witnesses when discussing their possible testimony is that I only want to hear the truth. If something they know may hurt our client's case, I say we may want to bring that out early to avoid letting the other side exploit what it will then call a "cover-up." If we don't plan on asking for that information ourselves, we prepare the witness to give a helpful, honest answer if asked on cross-examination.

Take Depositions

Depositions are a formal way of getting oral testimony from someone who may have helpful information about the case. Depositions are used to record the testimony of people the lawyers cannot informally interview (such as the adversary's witnesses) or to record the testimony of a witness who will be unavailable for trial. They are often used to pin down authoritative information from an identified company representative. Depositions can uncover what a witness knows or can confirm what he doesn't. They are also useful to show opposing counsel that a key witness (their own client, for example) may prove harmful to them at trial. Many cases settle shortly after a key deposition goes either very well or very badly. Depositions should establish exactly what a witness personally knows about a case. Lawyers often use depositions not so much to discover what they don't already know, but to pin down testimony so there are no surprises at trial.

Prepare to Settle

The prevalent thinking when I began practice was that whoever first suggested settling a case was displaying weakness and lack of confidence. I was taught to always let the other side begin that conversation. I no longer follow that advice. Since over 90% of all cases settle, I seldom hesitate to discuss settlement if the time seems right. It is never too early to consider a negotiated resolution. Every party needs to consider what a favorable resolution for them might be and whether it's worth starting a settlement discussion with the adversary. If the case can be resolved cleanly by a dispositive motion, settlement talks may not be useful until the theory of the case has been put to the test in court. No party wants to settle a case they can win, especially if the case can be won inexpensively by motion.

Some clients resist even discussing settlement possibilities because they have an unrealistically positive view of their case or because they believe they must take a stand as a matter of "principle." Principle is a malleable concept in litigation. The principle may be very clear at the outset of a case, but as the client continues to rack up costs and legal fees, principle tends to fade into the background as economics moves to the forefront.

Settlement discussion can be initiated by lawyers, clients, tribunals, or third parties. After a deposition or hearing, one lawyer may casually ask the other, "How can we resolve this thing?" Trials involve risk and expense on both sides, and a negotiated resolution can benefit each party. If it doesn't, settlement may be a mistake. Sometimes clients on both sides, independent of their lawyers, get frustrated with the legal process and begin to talk among themselves about how to work things out. Courts, having only limited time for civil disputes, want to clear their dockets. A court may order mandatory mediation – something of a contradiction in terms – to jump-start settlement. If the parties are far apart on terms, lawyers may suggest using a private mediator. Trained mediators recast the dispute in language that helps each party see the other's point of view. That itself is a giant step toward settlement.

Since most cases settle, the new lawyer needs to internalize the fact that settlement should be one consideration in the initial strategy of every case. Settlement may surface early or late, but the party considering its settlement strategy at each step of the litigation has the advantage. One barrier is that some clients lose confidence in a lawyer who raises the settlement option early on. They may feel the lawyer is not committed to the cause or thinks they have a bad case. To avoid putting off the client, the lawyer never has to use the word "settlement." It will suffice to explore the client's interests and values. Then, after becoming familiar with the interests and values of the adversary, the architecture is put in place to talk about other alternatives to solving the problem. The result is any time either party is ready to discuss settlement, the lawyer is prepared.

A common tension is how to negotiate settlement while simultaneously preparing for trial. Trial preparation can be all-consuming. Even taking a simple case to trial requires many decisions and hours of preparation. Who are the best witnesses to tell the story? What documents will be made exhibits? What will support or oppose anticipated objections to evidence? Witnesses, motions, and jury instructions must be prepared. Cross-examination of the adversary's witnesses is rehearsed. Opening and closing statements are prepared. And if settlement discussions are taking place at the same time, either trial preparation or negotiation strategy gets shortchanged.

To avoid this dilemma, some firms assign a lawyer who will have no part in trying the case to be their settlement manager. Trial preparation proceeds uninterrupted. Settlement strategies continue to be developed. But this is an exception to the more common practice that the same lawyer or team does both. In any case, it is essential that the parties come to terms with their absolute minimum settlement requirements before going to trial. Unless a settlement proposal is better than any other alternative, it should be rejected. Last-minute settlements tend to be more expensive because trial costs have already been incurred by both sides. While this may be unavoidable, it is seldom desirable.

Handle the Press

Because my wife worked in public relations when I was in law school, I came to believe that in a case that has public attention, it is better to talk with reporters than to have a news story conclude by saying, "The defendant's lawyer had no comment." The lawyers who trained me opposed this approach. They thought "no comment" was a victory. They had avoided saying anything overtly harmful. While this approach avoids misstatements, it also passes up the opportunity to shape what could be an unfavorable story into a neutral or even a positive one. Refusing to talk with the press means forfeiting the chance to reframe the story the public will be told.

Public relations professionals have taught me the value of taking an active role in presenting the client's story to an interested public. Even when I might want to keep a case out of the limelight, I want my client's version told first if there will be any story at all. When I have a case that may attract public attention, I hire public relations counsel. Then, when reporters call, I have a prepared approach that describes the controversy from my client's point of view. Even if the other side's point is well stated, ours is never left out.

New lawyers must tread carefully here. It's best to refer reporters' questions to the lead lawyer or to ask for the reporter's deadline so someone can call back. But if a reporter calls, there is an excellent chance a story will follow. Reporters are not lawyers' friends. It is important to agree at the beginning of the conversation whether the information offered is on or off the record or on background only.

Speaking with reporters always puts lawyers in a bind because it requires divulging information. The lawyer is squeezed between maintaining client confidences and helping the client project the most positive public image. Obviously, the client must approve the lawyer's speaking with the press. Equally obviously, everything the lawyer tells the press must be true. Lawyers are not under oath to disclose the whole truth, but if they lie to the press, the consequences are far more perilous than if they had remained silent in the first place.

Live With the Result

Most lawyers will admit they have lost cases they should have won and won cases they should have lost. Trial results are always uncertain. On any given day, any judge, jury, or arbitrator will get it wrong. The structure of the American trial system requires clients to make a very tough decision. Is it better to have the parties hammer out a solution among themselves, or is it better to hand the decision over to strangers who are limited by law or contract as to the range of possible solutions?

It is hard for the lawyer who has gone all-in on trying a case to just let it go if it ends with a bad result. All those late nights and cancelled events are gone forever. If the case involved a contingent fee, all that time worked was for naught. Some of the best lawyers are not very good at accepting defeat, but in the end, achieving a bad result is not the same thing as having done a bad job.

Takeaway Tips

Ponder the case
Prove the legal theory
Size up the opposition
Investigate the judge
Tailor discovery
Prepare witnesses
Take depositions
Prepare to settle
Handle the press
Live with the result.

CHAPTER VIII

Representing Clients

Learning how to develop a healthy lawyer-client dynamic will help the new lawyer build an enduring relationship. The key to establishing a successful law practice is becoming known as a lawyer who understands the client's problem and can solve it.

There is an adage that law is the perfect profession but for one problem: clients. This is not true, but sometimes it feels that way. We attract clients, do our best to satisfy them and get them to pay our fees, but some clients are just plain difficult to work with. They belittle our knowledge, challenge our every approach, or claim it is our fault when the path they insisted we follow leads to a dead end. Other clients resist honoring the fee or try to renegotiate it. Some clients are never satisfied, even when we work miracles. Yet sometimes our explanation of fees is imperfect, and sometimes even our best efforts fall short. Human nature operates on both sides of the lawyer-client relationship.

Many lawyers come to this profession because they want to be a part of changing the system. Sometimes a new lawyer is surprised by the maddeningly slow processes of the legal system. Change occurs one case and one client at a time. Even advocacy groups are limited by the opportunities to challenge a law or regulation. Change through law, however slow, is also real. The history of the Civil Rights movement in the United States is an example of that. Although still imperfect, civil rights in the United States is a far cry from what it was 50 years ago. But change came slowly, a case or a statute making only incremental progress. Every lawyer who dreams of becoming a change agent is limited by the goals of the client and the court's limited authority.

The opportunity for client representation is the single most important factor in defining the lawyer's career. We like to think our clients depend on us, and, in the matter at hand, they do. But in the bigger picture, we depend on clients to shape the pattern of our careers. Some lawyers are motivated by helping individuals or organizations. The client, not the issue, is their cause. The point here is that regardless of the lawyer's orientation, law practice is client centered. The lawyer who forgets that may burn out early or become disillusioned with the profession.

DOI: 10.4324/9781003533672-9

Serving clients is a privilege. This became clear to me a few months after I had left a prestigious law firm to start a small boutique. I was talking with one of my former colleagues at a local gym. He was bragging about how he was working for a power company on a lease of some nuclear reactors. The matter involved millions of dollars and had extensive press coverage. At the time, I was helping a small company that wanted to fire an executive. I was also representing a newly retired sheriff who believed he was entitled to a larger pension. In that locker room, I told myself, "You never should have left that big firm. He is doing sophisticated work, and you are not." I headed down the stairs to the street feeling sorry for myself. Then, halfway out the door, the realization hit me. His clients were assigned to him by the firm. Every client I had chose me. Suddenly, I felt proud. I had been asked by my clients to handle problems that would make a difference in their lives. I was not going to collect the same fee as my friend's firm would, but I had become a lawyer whom clients sought out. I am still thankful every time the phone rings.

Identify the Client

The first challenge is to determine who the client is. Obviously, if a lawyer is assigned to work on a project for a client, the person or organization being served is the client. However, in representing organizations, the identity of the client can become muddled. Principles of legal ethics[i] mandate that the client is the organization itself. While this is a fundamental legal concept, its application is not always straightforward.

Lawyers who regularly represent a particular organization often work with the same people in the company when legal issues arise. For example, a management-side employment lawyer will have regular contact with the client's director of human resources. As the two of them develop a solid working relationship, they come to trust each other. In the lawyer's mind, the HR director can become the client. Spending time in each other's offices, traveling together or sharing meals, they discuss personal or career goals and a friendship evolves. But the lawyer must always remember that the organization, and not his new friend, is the client.

All organizations have an internal political dynamic. Individuals push their own agendas. Departments within the client organization have internal rivalries that may not be readily apparent. Since lawyers have independent expertise, they can unwittingly be used by client representatives to advance their own personal or departmental agendas. For example, suppose the lawyer's main client contact has a favorite employee she wants to see promoted. She advocates her friend's qualifications to the lawyer, casting some shade on the other candidate. The lawyer, unthinkingly, affirms her choice. So, the representative casually tells her department head, "Our lawyer says we might have some legal exposure if we promote Sally instead of June, so moving June into the VP slot would expose us to less liability." Here, what might have been a lawyer's casual observation was taken out of context, mischaracterized as legal advice, and used to advance personal political goals rather than legitimate client objectives. It is hard for a lawyer to avoid these situations, but we should at least be aware they exist.

Welcome the Client

The best lesson I ever got on how to greet clients was from Fred Silver, a lawyer in Warren, Ohio. I was working as a summer associate in his firm before entering the Army. Fred's firm had a full staff and some of the lawyers routinely had staff members greet clients when they entered the firm and escort them back to the lawyer's office. Fred always got up, met the clients in the reception area, and walked them back to his office himself, while enthusiastically telling them how delighted he was to see them. His telephone manner was even better. No matter how pressed he may have felt that day, when a client called on the phone his tone and words let them know that their call had made his day. Fred made every client feel important. He could project a smile through a telephone. Emulating Fred's example lets clients know you care.

Listen to the Client

Listening is an art. Unfortunately, the unflattering description "fast-talking lawyer" is often accurate. If we have not listened carefully to understand exactly how the client sees the problem, there is not much we can usefully say about it. We may later conclude that the client does not have the full picture or is focusing on secondary rather than primary issues, but we cannot clarify goals and objectives until we fully grasp the client's perspective.

The first rule in listening is to let clients tell their stories in their own order, using their own words. Our incisive questions come later. If we direct the narrative, clients will always be reverting to their own version anyway. This impedes our ability to develop the facts into a plan of action. In addition, we will miss the emotional and social context of the story. Even worse, we may unwittingly replace the client's understanding with our own, unfounded, assumptions. Only once the story is fully told can we see how the facts disclose opportunities to solve the client's problem. Of course, there is a cost to letting clients tell the story their way. Not all clients can order events in a logical fashion, and some drown the narrative in their own verbosity. In these cases, the interview will be longer (and possibly more expensive), but the benefit of allowing the client to feel heard makes the rest of the lawyer's work easier.

The second rule in listening is harder to describe but equally important. Every client story has a text and a subtext. The subtext is composed of the thoughts, attitudes, emotions, and motives that underlie the words. Clients do not usually say, "I want revenge against the former employee I took years to train and who now is stealing my customers." Rational businesspeople do not like to admit being controlled by emotion. But the element of revenge may appear in the way they shape the story or in the gaping holes they don't fill. Careful listening will pick up this part of the story. When the lawyer later alludes to it indirectly, the client may then be more comfortable in admitting how he feels, which brings the lawyer another step closer to understanding the real issue.

Bear in mind that client stories change. They change because the client suddenly remembers a new fact or, becoming more aware of what may or may not be admissible in a legal case, sees the importance of a fact not disclosed previously. It is not unusual for a client to call and describe an issue and then, in the first meeting with the lawyer, recast the issue into something slightly different. Careful listening picks up these subtle shifts, which may change the strategy the lawyer ultimately adopts. Clients give lawyers information both by what they say and by what they withhold. Careful lawyers listen for both.

Uncover the Problem

The first question I ask in my Client Counseling class is, "Why do people come to lawyers?" It's a seemingly simple question, and the answers are usually some version of "Because they have a legal problem and need help."

We tend to assign the term "client" to people who come to see us. But thinking that way about the people who come to the office presumes they have an issue appropriately addressed by a lawyer. Yet the problem that brought with them may not be legal at all. It could have to do with a relationship, a medical condition, or simply an imaginary something that seems real to them. And if they do turn out to have an actual legal problem, that problem may not be what brought them in. A lawyer should never assume to know what the problem is or why the client showed up. Thus, at the outset, the lawyer must determine whether this is a person seeking legal advice for a problem a lawyer can professionally address.

To determine whether there is a legal problem underlying the client's issue requires some questioning. The lawyer must determine how the client views the problem, what the client wants to see happen, and what the facts are. Sometimes it is a challenge to figure out what the client really wants. Requests like "I want to incorporate my business" or "I want to buy out my partner" may seem straightforward enough. But before the lawyer starts to pull up different forms for organizing, dissolving, or selling a business, it is usually a good idea to slow down.

The lawyer should find out what kind of entity the business is now, who owns it, in what percentages and what business goals the other owners hold. Tax considerations may arise. Digging a little deeper may uncover an effort by one faction to gain leverage over other owners, to change percentages or to alter accepted decision-making processes. To effectively represent the client, the lawyer needs to know about all the principals involved, their relative ownership interests and contributions to the business and, to the extent possible, each principal's desires and goals.

Some clients know exactly what their goals are, some are uncertain, and some are embarrassed to admit them. Lawyers are not mind readers. We need to know the client's ultimate purpose, or we cannot help to achieve it. Clearly, making assumptions carries more risk than asking tough questions. Developing sophisticated legal strategies to solve non-problems is an expensive waste of time.

Some clients have unreasonable expectations. It is the lawyer's job to advise them if their goal is achievable and, if so, within what time frame. The law may not afford a remedy the client wants, or the process may require more time or expense than the client can afford. The new lawyer needs to expect that, by the time the initial meeting ends, the client may not have heard the lawyer say exactly what was hoped for. Here, the lawyer's attitude is critical. While being sympathetic to the client's aims and empathetic to the client as a person, the lawyer must not apologize for the legal process. Unless the client has been named as defendant in a lawsuit, there may be more effective ways to address the problem than through the legal system. Part of the lawyer's job is to suggest workable alternatives, though they may not be strictly legal processes.

One memorable incident brought this home to me, even as a relatively new lawyer. I had been practicing for almost a year in a large firm when I was challenged by the general counsel of one of our important clients. He wanted an immediate injunction in a labor dispute. The client had two separate businesses located adjacent to each other – a manufacturing plant and a trucking company. The plant's union employees had gone out on strike over a contract dispute, but they were picketing both the manufacturing plant where they worked and the main gate of the trucking company, which did not employ them. Union-represented truck drivers refused to cross the picket line at the trucking company, which basically shut down the entire trucking operation. As the general counsel saw it, this constituted an illegal secondary boycott. The other labor lawyers in our firm were all out of town and it fell to me, the new guy, to handle the situation. Under the "ally" doctrine of labor law, there was an argument that picketing could be lawful. I was not at all confident we could get an injunction, and the general counsel was calling every hour demanding to know when his company would get legal relief. Frustrated, I drove over to the trucking company and saw a group of picketers standing in front of a large truck parked just outside of the trucking company's main gate. The name and logo of the manufacturing company were painted across the whole side of its long trailer.

Seeing the general manager of the truck yard, I suggested he have a driver move the truck and trailer and park them in front of the manufacturing plant next door. The general manager was skeptical but went along with the idea. So, a driver climbed into the cab and slowly moved the truck away from the gate. It was just like a parade. All the picketers lined up, held their signs high and followed the truck until it came to a stop outside the manufacturing plant. It turned out they hadn't been picketing the trucking company at all. They were picketing the truck with the offending manufacturing company's name displayed prominently on its side. The problem evaporated as soon as the truck moved away from the gate. Even the general counsel was pleased. Moral: sometimes legal training can obscure common sense. Not every problem requires a legal solution.

A lawyer needs to maintain a positive attitude. This conveys he cares about the client, wants to solve the problem, is willing to evaluate all the available options, and will help select the one best suited to resolve the situation. Had the manufacturing client insisted on moving forward toward an injunction, the law firm would have billed for getting the papers filed, preparing for the hearing, and handling the hearing itself. Instead, this case was over the minute the picketers followed the truck. In the short term, the firm lost a litigation opportunity. But in the long term, it endeared itself to a long-standing client because the problem evaporated.

Develop Counseling Skills

It should be obvious by now that sometimes a client's problems are not optimally resolved through the legal process. This raises the issue of the lawyer's role in problem-solving when the problem is not essentially legal. That question presents a deeper one that cannot be ignored. What is the scope of law practice? Lawyers are not psychologists, social workers, physicians, or efficiency experts. Much of human endeavor lies beyond our ken. But my license to practice as a Virginia lawyer says I am an "attorney and counsellor at law." I read that in a very broad sense. Good legal counseling is more than simply presenting legal alternatives to clients and possibly advising them as to the best choices, given their own preferences and values. Instead, it involves bringing the whole of my professional experience to the problem at hand: how similar problems have been solved in the past and my experience in the workings of different industries.

Presented with issues plainly beyond my competence, I refer clients to physicians, psychologists, specialty lawyers, and public relations experts, among others. However, having practiced labor and employment law throughout my career, I have given advice on the behavior of groups, political strategy in handling union elections, and approaches for terminating employees. I have been hired to advise employers on improving dysfunctional management behavior and to coach managers on correcting discriminatory behaviors. All of these may seem outside the scope of law practice as such, but all fall within the skills acquired by experienced employment lawyers. Not to have acquired these skills over time would suggest a lack of expected professional proficiency. One client summarized the role he expected me to play in a union organizing campaign as being the "chief," coordinating overall strategy and directing other lawyers, business consultants, public relations counsel, and management employees toward achievement of the company's desired result. New lawyers, of course, would not be prepared to undertake such a role. But as they gain knowledge and experience over time, they will eventually be ready to do just that.

The role of lawyer as counselor differs depending upon areas of practice and scope of experience. But competent legal counseling involves more than simply advising on the application of law to particular facts.

Communicate Clearly

When I was still with the large law firm, one of my older friends, head of a large non-profit organization, came to my firm's estate planning group to revise his will. He was the beneficiary of some trusts set up by his father and wanted to protect these assets for his children and grandchildren. While his was a sophisticated estate plan, it was hardly complex. The next time I saw him, after he had met with his lawyer and signed his new papers, he said to me, "You know, I was in that man's office for an hour, and I did not understand a word he said." Apparently, the words the lawyer used to describe the estate plan to an intelligent client with an advanced academic degree had failed to communicate what the lawyer had done.

We lawyers talk to each other in legal shorthand all the time: "If you want a quick union election, file an 8(b)1(A) and an RM at the same time." Labor practitioners know exactly what this means, but it is useless babble directed to anyone else. Clients are not schooled in legal jargon. We must talk with them in everyday language – hardly a burden since there are few legal concepts that cannot be explained in plain English. If you achieve a reputation for speaking in plain English, you will attract more clients.

These same principles apply in writing to clients. Many lawyers forget that what the client cares about is what they want, not what the lawyer wants. Emails and letters should begin with something the client wants to hear: "You will be pleased to know . . ." or "As you requested . . ." are good ways to start. Client communication should focus on the client, the client's goals, and how this message fits in with the desired result. Even when the lawyer must deliver bad news, it is best to explain how the bad news fits into the overall strategy and emphasize what new options and opportunities arise, given this bad news. Only when a lawyer is writing to document a client's refusal to follow legal advice should a letter be written from other than the client's perspective. Clients want to hear what the lawyer is doing to help them.

When I began law practice as a labor and employment lawyer, I was taught to refer to clients as "we." For example, I would write, "If we are successful in . . ." This assured clients we were on their team. This usage, however, seriously annoyed the firm's corporate lawyers who preferred, "If the Company is successful in . . ." Our team's preference was to take every opportunity to identify ourselves with the client's cause so there was no question that we stood shoulder to shoulder. It may be characteristic of labor and employment practice that clients want to know their lawyer shares their orientation toward employees. On the other hand, while the corporate lawyers sought to show clients respect (note the capital "C" in "Company,"), they held a more detached posture to distinguish the law firm's advice from the corporation's decision. This simple example demonstrates the tension in the lawyer's relationship with the client. There is no universal right answer, yet it is critical not only to have a detached perspective, but also to show loyalty so the client knows that you personally care about their problems. If clients see you as a committed partner, they will return with other issues and refer new clients to you as well.

One of a lawyer's goals is to leave the impression that the lawyer, and the firm, would be valuable strategic partners for all future legal problems. If the client thinks you are only providing expertise for one type of issue, your opportunities for reengagement will be limited. Sometimes I am embarrassed when I think of the times a client hired another lawyer for a problem, not realizing it was one I handled regularly. What I had failed to do was communicate the scope of my own practice and the access I could provide to other lawyers, even if the issue was outside my own or my firm's expertise. It is not hard to build this kind of client relationship. It just requires communicating that you are dedicated to seeing their problems solved in the best possible way, even if that means referring the client to another lawyer outside your firm. If you can't be their lawyer in this matter, you want the client to know you will refer them to the best one possible.

Distance From the Client

While a lawyer may feel attached to the client, the lawyer must remain detached from the problem. Never forget, it was the client, not the lawyer, who committed the crime, married the spouse, signed the contract, or made the deal. Even when the client is an innocent bystander, the situation is not the lawyer's problem. The lawyer's problem is to navigate the best course toward resolution. When the lawyer identifies too closely with the client's problem or point of view, that lawyer loses that objective perspective the client needs most.

One of the challenges every lawyer faces is to recognize some adverse event for a client for which there is no effective legal remedy. While this is disheartening for the client, it demonstrates the lawyer's objectivity and builds trust. While it can be economically tempting to encourage the client's impulses to pursue legal remedies, affirming the impulse allows the client to be injured twice: once by the event and again by wasting time and money heading into a dead end.

Detachment is a gift the lawyer can offer the client. In representing terminated executives, I am invited into the job experience through the client's point of view. Every incident described is a story told to convince me that the client's decisions were right, her career was wrongly derailed, and she was undermined by jealous subordinates or misguided superiors. Most of my clients were able to describe, at least indirectly, the fault management found in their performance. But it always amazed me when, sitting at a small conference table in my office, I could observe the clients engage in the very same behavior that led to their dismissal. Had I embraced my client's point of view, I might not have seen the same reality the company managers did. A lawyer must listen for two stories: the one coming out of the client's mouth and the one supplemented by what the client is avoiding. Maintaining a sympathetic but detached point of view allows the lawyer to hear both sides.

Since the client's problem does not belong to the lawyer, the lawyer approaches the client's problem as an outsider. The lawyer is not committed to the client's version of the story and is free to discover an alternate version that also accounts for all known facts and reasonable conclusions. In contested matters, clients are normally under some stress and tend to get locked into their own narratives. Often, they are unable to appreciate even compelling alternatives that challenge or contradict their preferred version. By maintaining a detached mindset, the lawyer is free to allow each known fact to play its own role in developing the larger picture. Zealous advocacy does not require the lawyer to suspend judgment in favor of adopting the client's own bias. Rather, it frees the lawyer to re-conceptualize both the problem and the possible solution.

One risk to the lawyer's healthy detachment is spending too long working on the same case. Many years ago, I represented a young father who was doing construction work on an industrial site. Even though he fell 90 feet to the ground, he survived. His injuries were severe and permanent. A friend had referred him to me because he really needed help. Other lawyers had refused to take the case because of the workers' compensation bar, a legal doctrine that precludes an award of damages where workers' compensation benefits are available. I took the case because I thought I had found an exception to that rule that would permit a recovery of significant damages. As time went on, both my client's need for help and my commitment to his cause increased. I became more and more convinced that, at least in this one unique case, the exception to the bar would prevail. The more time I spent with him and the more legal research I did, the more I was convinced we could win.

The courts disagreed. Each round we lost I attributed to the court's not understanding how the narrow exception so perfectly fit these particular facts. Finally, when the Virginia Supreme Court refused to hear our appeal, we reached the end of the line. What started as the uphill representation of a severely injured man had become my personal fight for justice. Only after re-reading the lower court's opinion several times did it finally dawn on me that the courts saw our case as perfectly fitting the rule, not the exception. Concern for my client's well-being had become a shield that insulated me from the weight of the law. The lawyers who had refused to take the case were right. Even today, I do not regret that quest. It was not wrong to seek an interpretation of the law that bent in my client's favor. He needed an advocate and a friend. But I had lost my objectivity and became more like a Don Quixote than a wise counselor. Detachment would have helped me make better decisions, or at least make them with the blinders of righteousness removed.

When the lawyer becomes a true believer, neither the client nor the law is well served. Clients do not need cheerleaders; they need good lawyers. We do well to discourage them when they are tempted to act against their own best interests. But ultimately, unless we give them our best legal and practical advice from a detached perspective, we are not providing the professional service required.

Spot the Problem Client

Sometimes problem clients are identifiable at the outset of a representation, but even if a lawyer misses the early signals, difficult behavior may disclose itself early on. This is where the lawyer must have a well-drafted representation agreement. It should allow the lawyer to withdraw when continuing to represent the client becomes untenable. In litigation, withdrawal may require court approval. Some judges will not let lawyers withdraw except for the most compelling reasons – which might not include failure to honor a fee agreement. Many an unhappy, unpaid lawyer has endured a problem client for the duration of a case. It has taken me years to learn to rely on my own instincts. If there is something about a client that sparks a feeling of distrust or discomfort, the right decision may be to refer that client elsewhere. Sometimes you just trust your gut. Following this rule has given me much less heartburn than ignoring it.

Here is my personal list of clients to avoid.

Shoppers

Shoppers are sometimes hard to spot. On the phone, they say they want you to represent them. They may have sent you a document and expected you to discuss it in the initial phone conversation. But they never commit; they don't make a deposit to your trust account or return a signed representation agreement. What they are really doing is testing to see who will tell them what they want to hear for free. Shoppers are not clients, because they have not agreed to be represented. But they may have disclosed enough about their situation to require the lawyer to honor their confidences and preclude the lawyer from representing other parties in the conflict. In fact, don't think of them as shoppers; they are shoplifters.

Question-Askers

Closely related to the shopper is the question-asker. These would-be clients are not even shopping; they just want free legal advice. They only want to "ask you a few questions." But while questions in the abstract may seem harmless, all questions have a context and backstory. If you fail to gather that information, your answer will be misleading or, more probably, wrong. Some lawyers, notably those who practice in the personal injury area, may use question-answering as a technique for screening callers and qualifying potential clients. They do this for a purpose, and for them it is a useful practice. But generally, the best response is to suggest the caller make an appointment and come in for a consultation. Of course, it is appropriate to charge a fee for this. Hearing that a fee is expected, the caller will probably demur, saying all that is unnecessary because they just have a few questions. Lawyers are not free vending machines where people insert questions and receive answers. We represent clients. But your caller wants to "fill you in" so you can "just answer a few questions," and bit by bit, you learn information you must keep confidential. By indulging question-askers, you may have created a potential conflict without having an actual client. Answering questions via telephone, email, or text is a dangerous practice for most lawyers. Just politely maintain your willingness to help once the question-asker commits to becoming a client.

"Principled" Clients

Courts seldom decide principles; they decide cases. Neither do they enunciate principles to any client's complete satisfaction. Since most cases are settled prior to trial or final judgment, most cases never establish any principles at all. So, clients who bring a case to establish the principle of the matter generally end up dissatisfied. They want a court to declare their point of view as the reality to be accepted as a matter of settled law. They have no patience with factual and legal nuance, since these create ambiguity that throws a shadow over their cherished principle. Confronted with a legal bill that accurately reflects the cost of establishing principle, some clients back off, but not without expressing some sense of bitterness or anger. At this point, the principled client will complain about the pig-headedness of the adversary, the unfairness of paying legal fees, and the failure of our entire justice system. It is one thing to stand on principle and quite another to pay for it.

"Victim" Clients

Victimhood is in vogue, so the lawyer must distinguish between a person describing involvement in a traumatic situation and a person describing a broader, personal orientation toward life. People who adopt victimhood as an identity tend to be difficult clients – not because something bad happened to them but because they tend to believe that they are destined for bad things to happen to them. Any solution that falls short of confirming this client's victimhood undercuts their perceived victim status. Victim clients tend to be passive-aggressive, resisting decisions and deflecting responsibility. A victim may reject an otherwise favorable settlement offer unless it maintains their victim identity. This puts the lawyer in a difficult spot. If the client feels let down, the client may conclude he has been victimized yet again, and the new "victimizer" may be the unwitting lawyer who represented him. When this happens, the lawyer has an instant conflict of interest and needs to withdraw from the representation.

Clients who always need to be right share much in common with victimized clients. No matter what the facts show, no matter what the law provides, the client who is "right" rejects any result short of full vindication. New lawyers working in firms may not have a choice in avoiding these types of clients. When required to represent them, they need to document every step of the representation to protect themselves from these inevitably dissatisfied people.

Clients Who Change Lawyers

If a lawyer is approached to be the third lawyer to handle a matter, the general rule is: decline. Sometimes a client picks the wrong lawyer, so a change may be necessary. But when a potential client does this twice, the problem usually lies with the client and not with the former lawyers. A decision to decline representation is even clearer if the client complains about the former lawyers. If there is little choice but to take the matter, the best protection is a carefully tailored representation agreement. It should detail the expectations of the representation, the fee arrangement, and the lawyer's withdrawal rights.

Clients Who Do Their Own "Legal Research"

Sophisticated search engines and artificial intelligence make legal information available to everyone. On one hand, this makes the process of finding law easier. On the other hand, potential clients may draw false conclusions after reading cases, statutes, or regulations without understanding their content or context.

A discharged CEO once called me to discuss his "wrongful" termination. He was in his mid-sixties, convinced he had been let go because of his age. When he came into the office, he carried printouts of his own internet research. One stack of paper was the complete text of the Age Discrimination in Employment Act and supporting regulations. I listened to his story carefully. I told him I doubted he would be able to prove an age case since he had numerous documented policy disputes with the board of directors. Furthermore, he was 63 when the company hired him, and he had only been on the job for two years. He disagreed with my analysis. He was sure I had not fully understood his legal research. He questioned whether I was up on the latest legal developments he had discovered on the internet. He expected me to go through the Age Act with him, section by section, and explain why the words of the statute did not guarantee him a legal win. Our relationship never did cross into positive territory. I had to spend more time dispelling his imagined entitlements than exploring a viable way forward. Because this client had such easy access to legal information, he did not value my experience in knowing how to use it.

Disrespectful Clients

They do not respect your time, schedule, staff, or profession. They do not respect the representation agreement they signed. Their every whim constitutes an emergency, while your legitimate requests are an imposition. Your malpractice insurer will advise you not to sue them for unpaid fees. Fire them first.

Needy Clients

Some people are just more insecure than others. This may be their first time retaining a lawyer, so they are not sure how to navigate the process. Lawyers must spend more time with these clients to explain how and when things happen. There are many different styles of needy clients. Some have no one else paying attention to them and they begin to treat the lawyer as a friend-for-hire. Others are insecure people who come to depend on the lawyer for personal support as much as for legal advice. Some use extravagant flattery to keep the lawyer's attention. For others, the problem they brought to the lawyer may be a smoke screen, hiding other significant needs. One frustrated lawyer summed it up for me by saying, "I couldn't keep representing her. She wanted a mother, not a lawyer."

Needy clients may start out looking like good clients. They may sign the representation letter, keep their appointments, and pay the fee. Some of them ultimately develop productive working relationships with lawyers, but others do not seem to learn. They keep asking the same questions over and over, hoping to hear unequivocal reassurance. Their phone calls, emails, and texts become more frequent. Their comments begin to take on a passive-aggressive tone. They insinuate the answers are not coming fast enough. They seek certainty and resist ambiguity. The lawyer may then feel pushed into making assurances that exceed reasonable expectations. It can help to put the legal issue in writing and send it to the client labeled as a "status update report." The report may not change the client's behavior, but it does provide the lawyer with protection against any consequences of the client's growing disappointment.

Case Manager Clients

There are different legal theories on the extent to which clients need to be involved in case decisions. Ultimately, the case belongs to the client, who needs to be a part of all significant decisions. In litigation matters, some lawyers follow the rule that every substantive issue should be discussed with the client, but not routine, procedural matters. At any rate, the decision-making process should be fully discussed and agreed upon by the client in advance.

But some litigation clients are not satisfied to simply stay involved and participate in decision-making; they want to run the case. They want to dictate whether a routine extension request should be granted or how a routine email from opposing counsel should be answered. Frequently, their decisions are based solely on the level of irritation they believe the response will cause the adversary. For case manager clients, there are no norms of civility. Because they are paying the fee, these clients think the lawyer must do what they want, when, and how they want it. Any lawyer with a good reputation who represents this type of client will spend as much time resisting the client as working on the case. Confronted with such a situation, some lawyers just try to get the matter over with so they can be rid of the client. This may not serve the client's interest, because seeking prompt resolution to end the client relationship may prevent achievement of the client's optimal result. Here again, a clear, strong representation agreement at the outset can provide a solution. This document should stipulate that when the client repeatedly refuses the lawyer's advice or when lawyer and client are conflicted on strategy and tactics, the lawyer has the right to withdraw. Unfortunately, in litigation, court rules may affect a lawyer's right to step down. Sometimes there is just no way out.

Pseudo Clients

It is not unusual for people to seek advice from trusted friends when they make important decisions. From time to time, all of us consult with spouses, partners, friends, and trusted advisers before making big decisions. But now and then, a lawyer notices that the client resists making even routine decisions without first checking with someone on the outside. Here two different principles collide.

The first principal is common sense. Of course, everyone with a real say in the matter ought to be part of the decision-making process, because otherwise the decision may not stick. Mediators handle this problem all the time. They want the spouse, the trusted friend, or the insurance adjuster in the room so that when a deal is finally made, each has had a say and can sign off on it. The second principle, however, is attorney-client privilege. Fundamentally, everything a client tells a lawyer about a matter is confidential. Similarly, everything a lawyer tells a client about a matter is confidential.[ii] Yet it is perfectly proper, though generally unwise, for a client to tell a third party what a lawyer says. This privilege belongs to the client. Clients can waive this privilege but need to be advised of its risks.

When a client is dependent on a trusted adviser to help make decisions, the client may waive the privilege unknowingly. Most clients, when warned about this, keep the lawyer-client discussions to themselves. The dependent ones, however, may both disclose confidential information to the adviser and repeat what the lawyer told them. The obvious problem with this is that the client may have to answer deposition questions about what the friend learned, and the friend can be deposed about what the client said, thus giving the adversary an inside view of the case.

Outside of the harm caused by disclosing confidential information, having the trusted adviser outside the lawyer-client meeting slows the decision-making process and invites miscommunication. The lawyer can then advise his client to stop telling her adviser about the legal advice, or he can bring the adviser into the room so at least everyone hears the same thing. This move recognizes the adviser's role as a de facto client. It plainly waives the privilege, but it can also assist in decision-making. However, the client needs to be presented with the alternatives and the consequences to make an informed decision.

Parents of adult children represent one specific example of the pseudo client – and one becoming more common. Parents often believe they are the actual client, because in many cases, they are bankrolling the representation. They often pressure their young adult to include them in meetings, or alternatively, the son or daughter may depend on the parents' presence in the meeting. Parents may expect the lawyer to answer their own questions privately, outside the presence of the client. Often, the lawyer never gets to hear the client's total perspective. Parent presence inhibits any sharing of information with the lawyer that the adult child does not want the parent to know. All the lawyer can do here is to counsel the actual client – the adult child – about these risks, since the lawyer must ultimately abide by the client's decision.

Meetings where parents accompany adult children are inherently problematic. They take much more time than if the lawyer deals only with the client. The lawyer may think a decision was made, only to see it revisited after parent and child process the meeting on their way home. If an hourly fee has been set, the client or the parent may inquire why the bill is so high. Handling these relationships is both troublesome and expensive. Parents who expect to be involved should also expect to pay a premium for their involvement, commensurate with the additional time and complexity their presence occasions.

Delusional Clients

A friend referred a man to me who had just been let go from a large communications enterprise. He was in his mid-thirties, energetic and totally dumbfounded at losing his job. He was certain there was no rational reason for his termination other than a tangle with his boss over a work project. He was articulate about his plan to make the project succeed, how his boss had failed to understand his approach, and why, if upper management learned about this misunderstanding, he would be reinstated.

It puzzled me that, having worked for a large corporation for over ten years, my client did not grasp the simple concept that ultimately company leadership determines corporate goals, strategies, and standards of performance. So, I confronted him on this point. "Don't you understand that your boss, and his boss, who seems to be backing him up, get to call the shots here?" "No," my client replied. "That's not how this works. This is my project and I own this project. I'm the one who calls the shots on it."

For me, this was a novel exposition of the norms of corporate behavior. This unusual but clear response brought me to a new line of questioning. Apparently, his company, like some others at the time, was adopting the latest trend in getting employees to buy into corporate goals. The company wanted employees to take "ownership" of their work. This ownership idea had been presented in management training programs designed to empower employees to make decisions, unleash creativity, and commit to the work. "Taking ownership" was the new corporate cliché. My client obviously had taken ownership of the concept his employer had encouraged him to embrace.

While I tried to explain to him the law of employment, the concept of employment-at-will, the right of management to manage, and the futility of challenging its final decisions, my client simply said I was wrong. He said that I, like his boss, failed to understand that he owned the project. Much to his displeasure, I refused to adopt his fantastical view of reality, which, in fairness, had been instilled by his employer. The only fact he had to finally accept was his former employer's refusal to reinstate his employment. Ultimately, this unhappy client agreed to cede ownership by accepting a final separation agreement, thus ending his employment.

Here the intersection of a rigid personality with silly corporate jargon resulted in the employee's miscommunication with both his employer and his lawyer. Zealous representation requires the lawyer and the client to inhabit the same reality. It takes a large dose of patience to deal with a client who refuses to accept objective reality. Delusional clients have some characteristics of the principled client. They are not easily persuaded to approach their problem from any point of view but their own. They maintain their stance regardless of facts – which delusional clients tend to deny – or consequences. If their delusions cannot be overcome, these clients present an almost insurmountable barrier to the lawyer. Inevitably, they leave as dissatisfied clients.

We are not always successful in avoiding the problem client. But, again, having a good representation agreement in place that defines the parameters of the lawyer-client relationship is essential to making the relationship as productive and satisfactory as possible.

Client Billing Options

Those beginning to practice as an associate in a firm abide by the firm's established billing norms. But for lawyers with greater financial latitude, it is worth considering other invoice options. Clients expect to pay lawyers, but they are increasingly uncomfortable with open-ended billing arrangements. Sometime in the 1950s and 1960s, the way lawyers charged clients changed dramatically. The custom had been for bar associations to publish fixed fee schedules for typical services. These fee schedules were generally well received, except by anti-trust regulators who concluded they were a form of illegal price-fixing. Eventually, the fee schedule was replaced by the hourly rate for non-contingent fee work. Most lawyers embraced the change enthusiastically, because more complex matters could command a higher fee and all a lawyer's time could be compensated. Clients never liked this system, because they never knew the final cost of a case until after it had been completed.

Today, pushback against the hourly rate has resulted in some creative hybrid schemes that include consideration for time spent, difficulty, risk, and results achieved. Yet even as alternative schemes are widely discussed, hourly billing is still the norm. Time is irreplaceable. The irony is that hourly billing can reward inefficiency. Clients may be willing to pay a premium for value but not for time.

There is a wonderful story about a famous Washington, DC, lawyer and former Cabinet member. As the story goes, back in the 1950s, a client asked him a legal question and received a brief answer accompanied by an invoice for $100, a significant amount in those days. The client, disturbed by the high fee, sent a reply: "You just looked up this answer in a book. I need a more detailed accounting to support this fee of $100." The lawyer promptly complied. He produced a revised invoice: "Looking up answer in book: $1.00. Knowing which book to consult: $99.00." Knowing where to find answers is an essential component of the lawyer's craft. That knowledge is acquired through years of studying law, engaging in practice, and honing legal judgment. Few can deny its value. Knowledge, judgment, and wisdom justify a reasonable fee.

Takeaway Tips

Identify the client
Welcome the client
Listen carefully
Uncover the problem

Develop counseling skills
Communicate clearly
Maintain distance
Spot problem clients
Consider billing options.

Notes

i ABA Model Rules of Professional Conduct, 1.13.

ii The ABA Model Rules state in 1.6(a), "A lawyer shall not reveal information relating to the representation of a client unless the client gives informed consent, the disclosure is impliedly authorized in order to carry out the representation or the disclosure is [otherwise] permitted."

CHAPTER IX

Establishing Trust

I once knew a lawyer whose special gift was the ability to attract clients. While he was both skillful and clever, he didn't strike me as more than a competent, solid lawyer. But his stable of loyal clients was enviable. I asked a friend why that lawyer seemed to have such a thriving law practice. "Simple," my friend answered. "People trust him." Lawyers who inspire trust attract clients and build law practices. People go to lawyers when they have problems. They do not confide in people they do not trust. Nothing, I've learned, accelerates a lawyer's career opportunities like developing a reputation for trustworthiness. Trust is the glue that binds our social contract.

Early in my career, I lost a client's trust. I had been working on employment discrimination cases for a couple of years. By then I had reviewed hundreds of individual personnel files. They contained all sorts of sensitive, personal information about employees. My job was to see if those files had any comments about race or sex, which might disclose corporate patterns of illegal discrimination. For me, this was routine work, like gleaning good points from case digests.

One morning, I accompanied a firm partner to meet a client and investigate a new discrimination charge against this company. We met the company president and had a short meeting about the nature of the claims. While the president did seem a little prickly, I didn't think much of it. The partner asked if we could take some of their personnel files back to the office to look them over. When the boxes of files arrived outside their office, I opened the trunk of my car, pushed aside a snow shovel and blanket, loaded up the boxes and closed the trunk. The company president had a sour look on his face when I shut the trunk. He said, "Those are very sensitive files. Be careful with them." Trying to reassure him, I said, "No one will see them but us."

The next day, I was summoned by our firm's senior partner responsible for this client. "JB," he said," I'm sorry to tell you this, but the client doesn't want you to work on this case." I did not understand why. I had been appropriately quiet in the meeting and had done everything I was told. But it turned out that my casually tossing those sensitive personnel files in my trunk had offended the company president. Treating these files as no more than ordinary paper had made me persona non grata. The president must have thought he

DOI: 10.4324/9781003533672-10

was entrusting me with the secrets of his kingdom. Apparently, my casual approach to loading these boxes had crossed some invisible boundary. My nonchalance in this one small matter had eliminated any chance to build trust with this client.

While I still believe this was an unreasonable response, I have not forgotten the lesson. Each client has cultural sensitivities. Now, before I take any action, I try to scope out what those sensitivities might be. In this case, I should have noted that the files were delivered to me in a handcart pushed by an office assistant and personally accompanied by the director of personnel. Those files were being presented to me by the assistant, the personnel director, and the company president. Plainly, they saw this transfer as something akin to a ceremony of moving gold out of Fort Knox. My casual attitude toward this transfer and my failure to mirror the client's deference to the files tainted our relationship from the start.

One of the first questions lawyers ask about opposing counsel is, "Can that lawyer be trusted?" Trust among adversaries can be discerned reasonably quickly. Trustworthy adversaries are responsible lawyers. They keep their word and honor their agreements. They accommodate scheduling requests and press only those motions that make a real difference.

Even law firms develop reputations for trust. Some firms, deliberately or inadvertently, become known for "sharp practice." Determining whether a lawyer or firm can be trusted is a distillation of the experience of past encounters and transactions. Trust among adversaries is precious. Trust fosters candid conversations. From it flows disclosure of information that otherwise may have been withheld. Trust promotes efficient scheduling and streamlines litigation. Trust inhibits miscommunications and misunderstandings that impede problem-solving. Trust is the cornerstone of your career.

Honor Commitments

A person earns a reputation for trustworthiness – or lack of it – early on. The first thing the new lawyer can do to develop a professional reputation for trust is to follow through on commitments. Plan to arrive a few minutes early, never late. Turn in every assignment on time. Return phone calls promptly. Make it a habit to do what you said you were going to, which demonstrates dependability. Dependability engenders trust.

Use Discretion

The work I do every day can become routine. Things that are perfectly natural to me may seem threatening to a client. For example, when a client complains that a broker made inappropriate investments, the lawyer must collect information about the client's investment experience and personal assets. But asking people to disclose their net worth is not cocktail party conversation. Even if the client knows the lawyer well, he may be hesitant to disclose his assets (or lack thereof). Indeed, if the client and lawyer are friends, the client may be even more worried about how his friend views his wealth and what effect that will have on their friendship.

The lawyer needs to understand that asking certain kinds of questions may offend, raise sensitivities, or produce feelings of shame. These feelings are all barriers to trust. But since the lawyer needs the information to help the client, the questions are unavoidable. The lawyer's job is to make the client feel that the sensitive information is safe in the lawyer's hands; that the lawyer is not making any judgment about the client but is simply gathering necessary information.

It is human nature for people to avoid disclosing their most embarrassing moments or their most culpable behavior. Everyone wants to look good. Clients tell stories that soften or deflect the truth. Even transactional clients may be motivated by shameful impulses. They may be embarrassed that they want to take a larger bonus than their business partner because they feel they deserve it, while they feel their partner does not pull his weight. If a client seems to be covering up the truth, I will often say something like, "I know there are skeletons in the closet you don't want anyone to discover. But remember, I can't keep anyone away from those skeletons unless I know exactly where they are." Being prepared means doing everything possible to know what the client knows, while understanding the natural reticence to reveal that information.

Explain the Reasoning

One good technique is to interact like a teacher. When a client seems reluctant to share something, explain exactly how the information you seek will help them get closer to their goal. Lay out the legal theory and the known facts in ordinary language so the client has a sense of what additional information will be necessary to complete the picture. The best results come when the clients themselves realize how the information they are reluctant to disclose is critical to getting them what they want. Once they understand this, they may provide the information eagerly, feeling proud to have helped with their own case. Trust develops as they come to understand you are devoted to helping them solve their problem.

Once when I was representing a client accused of sexual harassment, I needed to find out some embarrassing details. I began by explaining the scenario he had presented in terms of the legal theory of sexual harassment, specifically that the conduct be "unwelcome" to constitute harassment. Once I had sketched the picture in terms of what behavior would suggest or refute welcomeness, he said, "Well then, you must need to know . . ." I never had to ask the sensitive question. The client volunteered the answer. Even if this optimal result were not achieved, explaining the reasons for questions makes the client feel like a partner in the process. This instills trust in both the process and the lawyer.

Keep Confidences

The American Bar Association's Model Rules of Professional Responsibility give lawyer-client confidentiality a very broad definition. Model Rule 1.6a states, "A lawyer shall not reveal information relating to the representation of a client unless the client gives informed consent, the disclosure is impliedly authorized in order to carry out the representation or the disclosure is [otherwise] permitted." This rule covers almost everything involved in representing a client, including the identity of the client and the fact of the representation. Some state rules, like Virginia's Rule 1.6 of the Rules of Professional Responsibility, are rather more limited. The Virginia Rule says, "A lawyer shall not reveal information protected by the attorney-client privilege under applicable law or other information gained in the professional relationship that the client has requested be held inviolate or the disclosure of which would be embarrassing or would be likely to be detrimental to the client unless the client consents after consultation."

The Virginia rule has three components defining information that must not be disclosed: (1) information legally protected by the attorney-client privilege, (2) information provided by the client that the client wants kept confidential, and (3) any information that would be embarrassing or detrimental to the client. A rule like this puts the burden on the lawyer to know the law and puts the burden on the client to tell the lawyer what to keep secret. There is no guarantee that the lawyer and client will agree on what may be detrimental or embarrassing, so the client needs to be clear on the subject. Obviously, to be informed, lawyers need to be familiar with their own state's confidentiality rules.

Probably the best practice for lawyers is to adopt the broadest view of protecting client information. In the context of representation, every client a lawyer sees, every fact a lawyer learns, and every conclusion a lawyer reaches should be treated as confidential. It is unnecessary to analyze each situation in terms of ethical rules if the lawyer makes this practice a professional guidepost. I do not talk about my clients with anyone outside my law firm. One consequence of this personal rule is that my wife has become upset when friends tell her that I have been helping them, but I never told her. Being told by the friend is the only way she will ever learn about my involvement.

At the outset of a representation, it is also important to remind clients that what they tell you – and what you tell them – should not be repeated to anyone else. Casual conversations with friends and family can result in the client's waiving the attorney-client privilege. People like to tell their stories to friends.

Some interpret the term "friends" rather broadly, including every person with access to their social media accounts. Comments posted on social media are not magically exempt from becoming evidence in court. Even when deleted, they still maintain a virtual life of their own. More than one workers' compensation claimant has lost disability benefits by posting videos of himself playing basketball.

There are real temptations to cross the lines described here. Lawyers love to talk. New lawyers want their friends and former classmates to know about the important work they are engaged in. But we must not identify a client or even give information that would lead to identifying a client. Think how the client would react if we were overheard.

Avoid Inadvertent Disclosure

There are many ways to err in dealing with confidential information. The first firm I worked for was in a high-rise office building containing other businesses and other law firms. Early on, I was instructed to carry files in the elevator with the client names pressed against my suit jacket rather than being displayed so everyone could see. I was told not to discuss client business in the restrooms or on the street. These simple rules reminded me that my work involves access to information that does not belong to me.

Some opportunities for disclosure are architectural. The many glass walls and glass doors in some newer law offices allow unobstructed views of who is transacting business with whom. Not long ago, I passed a law firm that put its main conference room on the ground floor of its new office building. The room featured floor-to-ceiling windows looking directly out onto the sidewalk and the street. Meetings there were visible to any passerby. What lawyer would hold a meeting in a room like that? Why would a law firm allow strangers to observe its client meetings and draw conclusions about the agenda just based on their possible knowledge of the cast of characters present? Perhaps the partners thought this presented an image of an open, unstuffy law firm. While new lawyers may not be able to control a firm's architectural taste, they can surely look for safer spaces to hold meetings.

Keep Notes Classified

Most lawyers take notes during meetings. Typically, this is a record of the basic facts: the main characters, their roles, the general situation, what the client wants to see happen, and any decisions made. I treat my notes as client confidences. They are scanned, put in the client's digital file in a folder labeled "Lawyer Notes" and protected by cloud security. The originals are shredded.

Sometimes lawyers receive information so sensitive that it should never be recorded anywhere. When a client tells a lawyer about marital infidelity, commission of a crime, or some act creating civil liability, it is prudent to omit these from the notes. Of course, this information is subject to the attorney-client privilege and cannot be disclosed absent client permission or court order. But supposing such notes are made, scanned, and filed. Where is the risk?

First, the notes become available to anyone who has access to the firm's files. Of course, they are all people covered by the attorney-client privilege who have a duty not to disclose anything they learn. But even assuming everyone honors that duty, including everyone hired or let go over the time those files are retained, more people will have access to that private information than a prudent lawyer should allow. Second, the client has a right to receive the file at any time during or after the representation. Lawyer notes, with some limited exceptions,[i] belong to the client. We call them "lawyer notes" only for convenience. So, a client asks for a copy of the file, takes it to the office or home and the information then becomes available to prying eyes. This poses a real threat to the client. A good general rule is that a lawyer should never record client admissions. While there may be necessary exceptions to this rule, failing to heed it is riskier than following it. I never had a problem remembering embarrassing facts or admissions when I needed to use them. I seldom discuss this information with a client again unless the conversation is unavoidable. Clients need to know they are safe. Safety builds trust.

Takeaway Tips

Honor commitments
Use discretion
Explain the reasoning
Keep confidences
Avoid inadvertent disclosure
Keep notes classified.

Note

i For a discussion of what information in lawyer notes may be withheld from a client, see 83 Colo. Bar Ass'n Ethics Comm Formal Op. 104.

CHAPTER X

Fixing Mistakes

All lawyers make mistakes, but it is how we deal with them that forms our character and builds our reputation. I was trained in a mistake-denial culture. In my first law firm, the operative rule was that mistakes could only be attributed to associates. Partners were exempt from mistakes. Even errors in strategic decisions, decisions seldom made by any associate, were often attributed to defective associate work. Obviously, this approach generates negative consequences. It creates a climate of distrust and defensiveness. It violates the principle that lawyers should be candid. It squelches creativity by valuing mistake avoidance over problem-solving. It sows suspicion and resentment among team members. A healthier approach accepts that mistakes are normal. Although we work to avoid them, creatively fixing mistakes is far more productive than blaming them on others.

We overlook critical evidence, misstate facts, misunderstand a client's desires, neglect our supervisor's directions, or even miss deadlines. We fail to trace subsequent case history only to have an adversary point out that our leading case has been seriously questioned, if not overruled. We inadvertently "reply all" and send sensitive information to the wrong people. We say the wrong thing to the wrong judge. We stubbornly adhere to failing strategies. In short, lawyers engage in ordinary human behavior.

Most mistakes fall into three categories: those we know we make; those others identify; and those no one thought were mistakes until they turned out to be. There is a fourth type of mistake, one based more on defective habits than simple errors. Sloppy proofreading and inattention to detail accumulate until they become significant mistakes. Indeed, they can become the most dangerous ones, because their repetition affects the lawyer's reputation far more than even one isolated error of consequence. Ultimately, they are failures of discipline, and the new lawyer must rectify that lack by patient determination and applying new habits. While all lawyers may not be naturally fastidious, every lawyer can learn to be.

DOI: 10.4324/9781003533672-11

Acknowledge Errors

The mistakes we identify ourselves are the easiest to fix. When we miss a deadline or forget an appointment, the best response is to deal with it immediately, without deflection or excuse. Some lawyers hesitate to admit mistakes. They imagine the error will be ignored or will pass without notice. But in an adversary system, mistakes tend to be discovered. A mistake admitted is already on its way to being remedied. Say, "I made a mistake and here's my plan to fix it." It's that simple. Just admitting you made the mistake and are already taking steps to fix it reduces collateral damage. Missing a deadline is not easily remedied, but the sooner it is addressed, the sooner it can be resolved. Admitting the mistake also allows others to suggest their own solutions, making a successful way out even more likely.

When someone else discovers the mistake before we do, the lawyer should adopt the same process: admit, take responsibility, find the best solution, apologize, and move on. Admitting mistakes seems disfavored in the current culture, but a lawyer's reputation depends on work that is consistently current and accurate. Mistakes not only detract from performance, but they also weaken the lawyer's brand. Admitting the mistake and taking steps to make it right goes a long way to restoring lost confidence. If the person uncovering the mistake suggests a fix, thank them, but make the correction that best solves the problem rather than necessarily adopting the one suggested. If the person identifying the mistake is a supervising lawyer, fix it the suggested way unless you can convince that lawyer of a better approach. We may be embarrassed by the error, but how we set it right will be remembered more clearly than what went wrong. In this sense, a mistake can be another opportunity to showcase good performance.

Two mistakes stand out in my Personal Hall of Infamy. The first, which still gives me chills years later, was more logistical than legal. I was negotiating a labor contract on behalf of a hospital several hours away from the office. After a long day of bargaining with the union and making little progress, I packed up my trial bag with notes, negotiation papers, and hospital pay information and headed for the hospital's large parking lot. It was dark and raining as I left. Finally arriving home, I got out of the car and flipped the seat to grab the trial bag – but there was no trial bag. I searched the car, the trunk, everywhere. Still no trial bag. I was close to panic. It then dawned on me that I must have put the bag on the ground to open the car door and just left it there when I headed down the road. All my client's secrets, to the extent they were in writing, were in that bag. If it fell into the wrong hands, I was cooked.

I phoned the hospital's security office. To my relief, a security guard had found the bag and brought it in. He assured me he would put it on a bus the next day and that it would be in town by noon. The next morning, after retrieving the bag from the bus station, I put a large greenback in an envelope and mailed it to the security guard who had saved my career. In the end, nothing was harmed except my ego.

My second worst mistake was *EEOC v. South Carolina National Bank*, 562 F.2d 329 (4th Cir. 1977). I had nothing to do with that case. I was not involved in any way, except that I should have paid more attention to it when I read it. My boss and I were handling a case in the Fourth Circuit involving the US Equal Employment Opportunity Commission and the doctrine of laches (unreasonable delay resulting in prejudice). In preparing our brief, I had read every laches case I could find. I found *EEOC v. South Carolina National Bank*, but I concluded it was completely off-point for our issues. So, I neither cited the case in our brief nor brought it to my boss' attention. That was the mistake.

During the oral argument before the Fourth Circuit, my boss was asked about that case and had to admit he was not familiar with it. The questioning judge, who had authored the *South Carolina* opinion, seemed rather put out: "That was our most recent laches case, and you don't know it?" I got an earful after the hearing. How could I have missed that case? The judge asked about it! Well, I didn't miss the case; it just had nothing to do with ours. But the circuit judge, who had written the *South Carolina* decision, obviously disagreed. I was embarrassed by failing to cite the Fourth Circuit's most recent laches decision. I should have cited it and said why it did not apply. While technically this may not have been a mistake of law, it certainly was negligent of me to neither cite it nor bring it to my supervisor's attention. Courts pay attention to their own cases, regardless of relevance. I should have known the court would be primed to ask about its most recent contribution to this rarely litigated doctrine.

To minimize the mistake's consequences, acknowledge what happened. There is no point in denying what will become obvious. A mistake denied has far more severe consequences than a mistake admitted. The Watergate affair taught that the cover-up can be far worse than the crime.

Admit Facts, Not Fault

There is an important distinction between admitting the facts of a mistake and confessing to fault. If the mistake creates serious consequences for a client, prematurely accepting fault may tie your malpractice insurer's hands. Admit the facts of what happened, accept responsibility where appropriate, but do not confess to fault. Leave room for the legal consequences to be sorted out by others. If the conclusion is that you were at fault, accept it and learn from it.

Put Client Interests First

The client will ask what you intend to do about the mistake. Your response requires your having thought this through completely. You may have formulated a plan to rectify the error. But was this plan developed to protect your client's interests or your reputation? Just asking the question discloses the possibility there may now be a conflict of interest with the client. If the client approves the plan to fix the problem and does not object to your continuing as counsel, you can go forward with the plan. But if the situation poses any tension between your interests and your duty to represent the clients' interests, you may have to withdraw and advise the client to seek new counsel. This is a tough position for any lawyer, especially a new one. Lawyers looking out for themselves first when fixing mistakes inevitably put the client in second place. If this happens, there may be no getting around the conflict of interest.

Notify the Insurer

Although it will add to your embarrassment, it may be necessary to inform your malpractice insurer. Today most malpractice policies are written on a "claims made" basis, meaning that the policy covers claims made or discovered during the policy period. Failing to inform the insurer gives the insurance company grounds to later deny the claim based on inadequate notice. The cost of embarrassment is far less than the cost of coverage denied.

Accept Responsibility for Everyone

The blame game is never worth it. If another lawyer is also at fault, that lawyer should also take responsibility. Their declining responsibility does not lessen your duty to accept your own. Not shifting blame is especially important when working with subordinates. At the end of the day, the lawyer is the one responsible for the work that goes out of the office. When an assistant makes an error, the lawyer takes responsibility for it. The lawyer's duty is to supervise assistants and oversee their work. So, any mistake an assistant makes must be treated as the lawyer's mistake. This does have one major collateral benefit. When the lawyer protects the assistant from blame, the lawyer gains personal loyalty from the whole administrative staff, not just the assistant. This offers huge rewards in the long run. The reverse is also true. When a lawyer blames an assistant, the staff loses trust in the lawyer. Shifting blame deepens the pool of resentment, guaranteeing later negative consequences. Even if it feels unfair to accept full accountability, softening the blow for teammates pays future dividends.

Find a Solution

Figure out how to solve the problem. You may be surprised by how often opposing counsel will accommodate non-fatal mistakes. Other lawyers know they may need similar accommodation in the future. Ask your team or other lawyers for their ideas. Sometimes just considering the problem from a different perspective opens the door to a more creative solution.

Learn From Mistakes

After discovering a significant mistake, it may be time to revisit your decision process. What did you overlook that allowed the mistake to occur? If it was a time deadline, how is your calendar integrated into your task list? If it was deficient research, retrace your steps and find the turn you missed. If it was a rule of court or part of a pre-trial order, were the requirements integrated into your calendar process? Find the weak spot. If following your normal process would have avoided the mistake, continue the process. If not, improve the process.

There is a boundary between analyzing a process and over-analyzing it. Sometimes a supervisor will ask, "What have you done to assure it won't happen again?" This may be just a passive-aggressive way of saying, "I don't trust your judgment," or it could be an encouragement to think the process through again. The tendency of the over-careful lawyer is to create so many protective rules that mistake avoidance becomes a form of paralysis that makes any project take longer and cost more. This habit saps energy. Mistakes are expensive, but creating a maze of processes to avoid a slip can be even more costly.

Once I represented nine individual defendants in an employment non-competition case. Each one was sued and served separately. I thought I had filed nine answers, one for each defendant. As it turned out, I had only filed eight. The judge held a hearing in chambers on the plaintiff's motion for default judgment on the one case for which I had failed to file an answer. After plaintiff's counsel had explained why his client was entitled to judgment by default, the judge turned to me and said he didn't want to hear an argument, he only wanted the answer to one question. "Mr. Burtch, he said, did your client fail to give you the complaint he was served, or did you fail to file an answer? Was it his mistake or yours?" I replied, "It was my mistake, your Honor. I left one out when I filed the other answers." "Well," the judge said, "if it was the client's mistake, I'd find him in default, but since it's yours, we'll just forget about it. All lawyers make mistakes."

There is no benefit to carrying around a career's worth of mistakes in your brain. They will be there as reminders when you need them, but otherwise, let them go.

Takeaway Tips

Acknowledge errors
Admit facts, not fault
Put client interests first
Notify the insurer
Accept responsibility for everyone
Find a solution
Learn from mistakes.

CHAPTER XI

Surviving Office Politics

My first job as a lawyer was with the largest law firm in Virginia. However, during law school in Nashville, Tennessee, I'd worked at two different firms. Then, after graduation and awaiting entry into the Army, I worked at a firm in my home state of Ohio. Each of these three firms taught me something important about being a lawyer. What surprised me was that this education came as much from the firm's staff members as from its lawyers. The lawyers taught me to produce work they could use. The staff taught me to fit into the firm's system. Success as a law clerk meant keeping both lawyers and staff happy. I was fortunate to have this early introduction to law firm culture before I started my first full-time legal job.

When I arrived, the Richmond firm was in a growth spurt. As a result, there was no office available for its newest associate, so I hung out in the back room of the firm's law library. Those were the analog days of law practice. There was no phone and no Dictaphone (an early recording device similar to a mobile phone's voice memo function). The library was far removed from the other members of my team.

Some library users resented my presence because I'd taken over the only private workspace in the library. However, the librarian was happy to have me. He collected firm gossip and was glad to have a confidant. We became friends, and when he finally got an assistant, I became friends with the assistant. Over the years, knowing those two men served me well. Even long after I had left the firm and the librarian had retired, the assistant still provided me with access to resources I could not find anywhere else.

Not having a Dictaphone slowed my work production. The office manager told me there was no budget for one of my own. When I presented the problem to our section head, he took a long pull on his unfiltered Camel cigarette and said he knew I was a resourceful young attorney, so he was sure I could find one. I took that as permission to remove one from a tiny dictation room in the library, and I kept it with me my whole time at the firm.

Associates accumulated office furniture in much the same way. An associate had only to announce his impending departure and scavengers would arrive in his office to cart away client chairs, small tables, and bookcases that they used to upgrade their own space. I suppose this style of refurbishing suited the firm's budget. It also served as a rite of passage for those about to leave.

 DOI: 10.4324/9781003533672-12

Most law schools don't teach a course in office politics. It is learned by trial and error – mostly error. In today's world, equality and equity are important values. So, it probably violates all rules of politically correct expression to observe that many law firms still operate according to a caste system. Firms are either explicitly or implicitly hierarchical.

Once, it was not unusual for firms to list lawyers on their letterhead by name and order of their arrival. The most senior lawyer was listed at the top and the most junior at the bottom. Sometimes there was a line marking the division between partners and associates. Lawyers crossed the line as they were promoted. Should an associate with less time at the firm become a partner, that associate would then advance to the bottom of the partner list, and it would be obvious who had been passed over.

This system had a certain practical brutality. Associates knew where they stood. The lists disappeared when firms became so large it was no longer feasible to put every lawyer's name on the letterhead. The pecking order, however, has not disappeared. Partners and associates (including all the other categories now used to disguise lawyers who are not owners) usually know exactly where they stand. Law firms have remained caste systems because traditionally there have been only two classes of employees: lawyers and non-lawyers. Non-lawyers, the lower caste, are described by what they are not, as opposed to what they are. They may be distinguished CPAs, award-winning marketing specialists, and campaign-winning political consultants, but they are *not* lawyers. The newly hired, most junior lawyer becomes a member of the higher caste, regardless of actual value to the firm. While this situation may not be reflective of the real power relationships within the firm, most firms still cling to these distinctions, even though they foster resentments.

One antidote to this caste system is the multidisciplinary practice, which is now common in Europe. Internationally, multidisciplinary practice is more efficient because it allows professionals with different areas of expertise to advise clients as well as better access to capital to finance growth.

In a firm with highly trained, non-legal professionals and long-term staff employees, this caste system causes significant tension. Sometimes a senior assistant – who may have played a critical role in the firm's success or had a strong relationship with an important client – may be excluded from conversations about client strategy simply because she does not have a law license. To this extent, the caste system excludes some who could add value to the conversation.

Cultivate Allies Among the Staff

Staff can make or break the careers of new lawyers. As the newest lawyer in a large firm, I stepped into a world of complex relationships that determined much of the firm's daily operation. None of this power dynamic was reflected on any organizational chart. Miss White, who never had a title as far as I could tell, told me where to park, where to open my personal checking account, and how to get airline tickets and travel advances. Mr. Sawyer ran the office services department. They printed and bound every brief I filed in court. All requests for legal pads, pens, clips, and staples went through him. Anything that had to be copied, printed, bound, shipped, or delivered went through his staff. Meeting a deadline was simpler if you followed his process rather than attempting to impose your own.

Miss Kovac ruled the records department. A short, solid woman with a love of country music, she ran records like a master sergeant. Her loyal staff looked for her signal on how to meet a lawyer's request. Being on her good side made files appear like magic. Anyone brave enough to test her patience saw her other side. I learned I'd made it in her eyes the day I walked into the records room and stood there waiting to get someone's attention. When Miss Kovac noticed me, she shouted at one of her staff, "Frankie, get off your fat ass and see what Mr. Burtch wants." She was both direct and offensive, but I left with the files.

Mrs. Rogers presided over what we then called the secretarial staff. She decided which staff members were assigned to which lawyers. Any private conversation with her began with her lighting a long Virginia Slims cigarette. Before the rules got too complicated, she also functioned as the firm's de facto personnel department. Once, when she thought the secretary for the firm's usually absent senior partner did not have enough work to do, she assigned that secretary to help me get emergency injunction papers filed, even though that secretary hadn't typed a pleading in 20 years. What I learned from these strong personalities was that regardless of the demands and expectations of my lawyer-supervisors, getting anything filed and out the door required the cooperation of all these teams. If you made them your allies, it could be easy; if not, you crossed them at your peril.

The digital age has not erased the power of individual personalities. Any law office has people who can make a lawyer's work easier or more difficult. Every law office has its own dynamic and internal politics, and the quicker the new lawyer figures out the lay of the land, the easier it will be to succeed at the job. New lawyers sometimes assume that office politics are distractions that do not affect them. These lawyers operate as if they are above it all, which simply makes them targets to be brought down. If everyone in an organization were pulling in the same direction and all energy were focused on serving the client, a discussion of office politics might be unnecessary. But no organization is so perfect that personalities and strategic alliances aren't part of the office dynamic.

The concept of working space has evolved as well. Today a lawyer's office can be almost anywhere. Some lawyers practice out of backpacks in coffee shops, others in shared workspaces, others alone at home, and still others from cell phones in their car. But no matter where lawyers work, if there is more than one person in the organization, office politics creeps in.

Some staff members believe they are entitled to more authority or deference than others. They may be the ones with the most seniority or those who work for the senior partners. The new lawyer needs to get to know these employees but, at the same time, keep them at a safe distance. At first it may not be apparent what real power they have. The general rule, of course, is to treat everyone with courtesy and respect, regardless of status. But within a few weeks, the new lawyer should be able to identify the real staff power brokers.

Offices have become more democratic than they once were. Today, no one expects an assistant to bring coffee to the boss. Lawyers are expected to serve themselves and clean up afterward. The first firm I worked for had a maid, formally dressed in uniform, who circulated around the office bringing coffee, picking up cups, emptying ashtrays, and straightening conference room chairs after meetings. Those days are long gone. It's bad economics and worse optics.

I shared my first secretary with a senior partner who spent most of his day talking on the phone and drinking coffee. He would dictate letters and occasionally leave the office to see a client. Our secretary knew this partner approved her raises and vacations, so I was left to grab any time she was willing to spare. In her world, keeping her partner's coffee warm was far more critical than producing a pleading for me. I used to practically beg her to get any of my work done. My situation improved when our section hired another new associate. Because of my good relationship with Mrs. Rogers, I got to share a secretary with the new associate, and I became the senior – and favored – member of that small team.

Let Staff Members Train You

Senior lawyers train new lawyers about job expectations and how to practice law. But the process of getting the work in final form and out the door is best learned from the staff members who make it happen. Experienced assistants are usually willing to teach new lawyers if the new lawyer has sufficient humility to learn. Assistants hate micromanagement, especially if it is being done by a lawyer they don't think understands the process. Early on, the new lawyer should have a frank conversation with the assistant about how best to work together.

Lawyers also need to understand when to back off. I learned this the hard way. One day after lunch, I'd persuaded a partner's secretary to help me get a pleading filed that same afternoon. Since I was very anxious about it, I wanted to be sure it was being done right. So, I stood beside her desk while she was typing it up. I'll never forget the moment she stopped typing, looked directly up at me, and said, "JB Burtch, if you don't get back in your office right now, this pleading will never get filed." My anxious micromanagement was not helping her work. She knew what to do, and she got it done.

Assistants can be invaluable in improving letters and briefs. One of the downsides of working on a single matter for a very long time is that lawyers tend to see the problem from only their own perspective. Listening to clients, reading their documents, developing legal theories, and researching the law tends to produce a view of the case biased in the client's favor. One reason sophisticated clients hire a different firm to handle the appeal of a case is that the original firm has probably bonded to its original theory. Fresh eyes with a different perspective may find a more creative path to a successful result. An assistant can perform a similar service. The assistant can read a brief or a letter and tell the lawyer whether its point is clear and makes sense. If my assistant was not convinced by a brief, or even missed the main point, I knew it needed more work. Often assistants can provide a judge's-eye view of a case that another lawyer cannot. Judges don't spend all their time absorbed in one case, nor do they read a brief in the same context a lawyer writes it. If your own assistant is too close to a case, ask a different assistant to read the papers. If an intelligent assistant comes away unconvinced, the draft needs revision.

Assistants also see things lawyers don't. For some years, I did the screening interviews for lawyers or law students applying to our firm for jobs. With me, these applicants were always on their best behavior. After I had escorted them back to the elevator, I'd ask our receptionist for her impression. Reactions ranged from "She's wonderful; you should hire her" to "If that guy gets a job here, I'm leaving." I was always amazed when applicants didn't have the sense to know that everyone in the firm had a stake in their hiring. Applicants are evaluated by everyone they encounter. Arrogance at the front desk is a sure offer-killer.

Anticipate Family Dynamics

Law offices behave more like clans than businesses. Maybe that's because the partnership form of organization encourages a more familial kind of relationship. Whether a firm is a true partnership or one of the many corporate substitutes (LLP, PC, etc.), most tend to behave like partnerships. The defining characteristic is that partners (or members or shareholders) in a law firm believe that they, in fact, are owners of the entity and thus entitled to influence every firm decision. Thus, while rivalries and factions are present in all businesses, in law firms they may have an added emotional dimension.

Shortly after my arrival at the firm, a memo went out announcing that Mr. Jones had withdrawn from the firm's litigation section. Attached was a list of clients and files that hereafter would be handled only by him and his associates. I asked my boss what was going on. It seems that Mr. Jones, a renowned litigator and austere Baptist, tangled regularly with the head of the litigation team, a cigar-chomping Catholic, and things had finally come to a head. A few weeks later, another memo appeared, cancelling the first one. Apparently, the rift had been smoothed over. In any rational business, this behavior would not be tolerated. One department cannot simply secede from the organization and expect to survive. But in many law firms, some partners believe they are entitled to run their law practices any way they want. This, of course, flies in the face of modern practice management.

In a profession that operates at the very heart of the adversarial system, it should come as no surprise that some people just don't get along. It's not the new associate's job to become the organizational consultant or to fix broken relationships. But it is the new lawyer's job to survey the territory. Becoming familiar with the webs of alliances and rivalries in a firm will make the new lawyer more secure. What groups go out to lunch together or mingle after work? How are the offices arranged? Who works together and who works separately even though it makes no functional sense? What are you intuiting from staff's casual comments? It is ironic that some firms will finance partner retreats where they define their mission and goals for the year, while at the same time they sustain an organizational culture that devalues common goals. The new associate is not going to pick this up all at once, but figuring out the basic office dynamics will help that associate avoid unnecessary conflicts.

Observe Firm Leaders

When I'd been a member of the bar for only two months, I had lunch with the managing partner of a national law firm. He was the father of a former school roommate and a mentor of mine. I'll never forget what he told me about his vision of law firm governance at that time: "We have to run our firm the way they run General Motors. A firm must be led by a strong executive team. You can't have a successful law firm with each partner running their own agenda." The new lawyer does not have to become a guru on law firm organization, but he does need to pay attention to the goals of his firm leaders. It will advance his career if he has some sense of where the market he serves is moving, how his firm is responding to it and how to become a chosen provider for that market. It is never too early for new lawyers to become aware of their own role in a changing economic culture, so their career decisions will be informed by the economic forces influencing the firm and the profession.

Thus, it is important for the new lawyer to understand how the firm operates, how it defines its purpose, and who is in charge. With a little curiosity and a lot of observation, the new lawyer can begin to see who makes the critical decisions. In a large firm, there may be a president or chair or executive committee, or even all three. Are these the people respected and deferred to, or is there a hidden cabal of lawyers who call the shots? Is the team or section seen as critical to the firm's mission, or is it a support function that backs up the front-line teams? Is the group profitable or marginal? Is the team leader a firm leader, an emerging leader, or not really part of any decision-making group? Just having these questions in the back of the new lawyer's mind makes that lawyer more observant and perceptive about the firm's future and her role in it.

It is hard to overestimate the amount of time disorganized law firms waste making decisions. Unless the firm has a decision-making structure that empowers the leadership to act, decision-making becomes an ever-shifting, never-ending exercise in consensus building. Factions that disagree with firm goals try to renegotiate issues others think have been resolved. Generally, the new lawyer will not be involved in these internal machinations. But she will want to know if this is a firm she can commit to – and which will commit to her. Should it become apparent that much of the partners' energy is spent on internal firm politics rather than serving client needs, the new lawyer has valuable information for future career decisions.

Evaluate Firm Friendships

People who work together day after day on critical matters in close quarters tend to develop what they believe are real friendships. While we may not put our friends at work in the same category as our other friends, it is not unusual to feel personally close to some fellow employees. Yet these friendships may prove to be only transactional. They begin in the workplace and are nurtured by achieving common goals. But if the work relationship changes, the friendship may turn out to have been nothing more than a close and comfortable alliance. When you join a firm, expect to make friends. But also expect that the relationship will be affected by the needs of the organization as much as by the affinity of the individuals. You may find a soulmate at work, but it remains to be seen if the relationship ultimately survives the job.

This raises the subject of romantic relationships at work. People fall in love at work every day. Doctors marry nurses; bosses marry assistants; partners marry associates. Falling in love with someone at work is always complicated, sometimes painful, and often fatal to a career. Workplace romances tend to go in one of two directions: marriage or south. When they move south, there will be drama, accusations, suspicion, jealousy, and work disruption. There may also be termination of employment followed by litigation. The simplest strategy is to steer clear of romantic involvement with anyone at work. Today, office romances are dangerous. If you fall in love at work and the feeling is mutual, the safe move is to find another job if you want to continue the romance.

A significant part of my law practice has been devoted to representing individuals accused of sexual harassment in the workplace. There is a fine line between a consensual sexual relationship and sexual harassment. People in love (or just on the make) may perceive reality differently than the object of their attraction. Feelings change. What was once a welcome mutual dalliance may come to be seen as sexual harassment. No matter how discreet the couple may want to keep the arrangement, co-workers usually figure out that something is going on. The powerful human emotions involved are difficult to hide from the people who surround you every day. I was once asked by my firm to ascertain whether one of our lawyers was having an affair with his office assistant. Since I didn't have any firsthand information, I queried our office messenger. He was a perceptive man whose job took him all over the office. "No question, JB, they are involved with each other." Taken aback by the certainty of his answer, I asked how he could be so sure. He said, "Because he acts so jealous any time her husband calls." The couple would have been surprised to know that the firm messenger had such a clear take on their situation.

Be Wary of Office Parties

Office parties have their own perils. My father's advice was that there is no office party worth attending. The first time I heard that, I thought he was a real killjoy who wanted to spare the expense of throwing a nice party for his staff. But after I had worked in more offices, I came to see his point. Some events can be relatively harmless, such as a leader taking a team out for lunch or drinks. Assistants and lawyers can then interact in a way they don't at work, get to know each other in a different context, and sometimes establish a good feeling that carries over and makes working in the office more pleasant for all. But alcohol loosens lips. Otherwise harmless gossip leads to sharing confidences, speculation, and resentments. The wrong thing gets said and a relationship is ruptured. Since it is a work relationship, it may have an economic consequence as well.

My strongest office party memory was being a guest at a client's big holiday reception. All their staff, vendors, and good clients were gathered, filled with holiday cheer. Toward the end of the evening, one employee, well into his cups, approached the company's CEO and took the opportunity to let him know exactly what needed to change to make the company a better place to work. His views were offered at a volume that allowed everyone to benefit from his advice. Although the CEO maintained a polite composure, he was clearly embarrassed. The next morning, I got a call from that CEO asking me to draft a termination agreement for that helpful employee. His behavior at the party had ended his career there.

For most people, office parties without alcohol aren't much fun. With alcohol, however, they are gasoline waiting for a match. Taking a group to a nice restaurant for lunch is a much better solution for celebrating holidays or milestones. But if the big party is a command performance, the best strategy for the new lawyer is to arrive on time, make the rounds to be seen, and as soon as decently possible, quietly disappear into the night.

Some will bristle at the idea that working successfully within a law office requires a level of political savvy, but no one should be surprised. Every office in every industry has the same challenges. Successfully navigating the minefield of personalities and conflicting agendas in a law firm requires understanding the political tensions that will influence the new lawyer's career.

Protect Your Career

A former associate of mine secured a job with a large, nationally respected law firm. The firm assigned him to a team led by a partner with no influence in the firm. After several years of performing outstanding work but receiving no recognition, he chaffed at being stuck in a backwater. The firm's politics prevented him from switching sections so his legal talent could be put to better use. Ultimately, he concluded his only option was to leave that firm. Today he is a star. He became the in-house general counsel of a highly profitable enterprise. His former firm never got to collect on its initial investment in his career because they were not flexible enough to move him into a role where that investment could pay off.

Even if the new lawyer's first assignment is not ideal, it may be possible to migrate within a firm to a role with more opportunity. If the internal barriers prevent that, as they did with my former assistant, you may have to seek opportunity elsewhere. Not all lawyers, however, are motivated to climb to the top of a firm's ladder. Many find satisfaction in developing specific areas of legal expertise. There are different paths to success within a law firm, but most lawyers are happiest when their career paths are determined by their own choices rather than by a happenstance of fate.

At the outset, the new lawyer should figure out if his firm's lawyers work together as an intentional unit or just as a collection of different practices under the firm's name. This can define the path to advancement. Most lawyers have strong egos. Each believes he is the keystone of the firm. Trying to organize lawyers is like trying to herd cats: they resist being led. Each has his own vision of what he wants to do for the firm and what he wants the firm to do for him. It takes strong leaders to convince a group of intelligent prima donnas to subordinate their individual desires to the firm's vision. If the organizing principle of the firm is simply to contain autonomous teams of good lawyers, a core vision may not be as important. It makes a difference which type of organization the new lawyer joins. Either your path will be dictated by the firm's leadership, or you can chart your own course. Having a clear sense of your own organization gives you more control over your future.

Takeaway Tips

Cultivate allies among the staff
Let staff members train you
Anticipate family dynamics
Observe firm leaders
Evaluate firm relationships
Be wary of office parties
Protect your career.

CHAPTER XII

Staying Sane and Solvent

Remain Balanced

The law is a high-stress profession. Despite all the jokes about our ruthlessness, avarice, prevarication, and aggressive persistence, the simple truth is that we are hired to advocate causes. Unless we can choose the causes we represent, we find ourselves caught in the inevitable conflict between our clients' desires and our own. There is just no way around this if we are to represent members of the public. We champion causes that may conflict with our own values. Clients bring us problems they can't solve. We spend our time on their problems, often ignoring our own. Thus, the very work of lawyering necessarily creates stress for the lawyer.

Psychologists have a term for this: cognitive dissonance. We endure cognitive dissonance every time we fight for a client's goals that conflict with our own beliefs. Inevitably, we pay a price. The cost may be imposed on our bodies, minds, or souls. How the lawyer deals with this inherent tension may determine his physical or mental well-being. Lawyers suffer from depression, drug addiction, and alcoholism in far greater proportion than the general population.[i]

By shouldering clients' burdens, we insulate our clients from dealing with their own legal problems and insert ourselves into the breach. We use our expertise and knowledge to solve those problems, or at least to get our clients in a better position to address them. But it is dangerous to carry another's burden as if it were our own. We must maintain a sense of balance. When their problem becomes a problem we carry personally, the scales have tipped, and we've lost balance.

Maintain Emotional Distance

Once it was common to speak of the lawyer's role as providing "detached legal advice." The phrase conveyed the notion that while we were to be empathetic with clients and sympathetic to their situation, we could not be useful if we became personally attached. If we did, we would never see the problem objectively – a prerequisite for giving solid legal advice. Once engaged, the lawyer

 DOI: 10.4324/9781003533672-13

cannot afford to be either too attached to the client's cause or not committed enough. Either posture deprives the client of an objective, zealous advocate.

After I left a large law firm and had to find my own clients, I took some cases I should have avoided. Several of these were divorce matters, for which I do not have the temperament. I resented clients who felt I did not show the antipathy for their spouses they assumed I should have. It baffled me how a person who at one time had committed his life to the other, now saw the former beloved as a present anathema. Custody and visitation issues seemed to become opportunities for financial leverage rather than opportunities to maintain relationships with children. I have presented divorce clients with settlement proposals from the other spouse – which ethically I am bound to do – and then been accused of having sold out to the other side. Some of these clients seemed more motivated to hurt their former spouses than to live in peace. I concluded divorce clients were all impaired, at least temporarily. This attitude protected me from accepting reality on their terms. Too close an identification with the client's attitude leads to sloppy legal advice.

The concept of detached legal advice seems to have fallen out of favor. One of the texts I have used for many years to teach Client Counseling in law school may suggest part of the reason detachment is no longer in vogue.[ii] The Binder text advocates "client-centered counseling" as a way of "empowering clients to make decisions they consider satisfactory."[iii] According to Binder, while a lawyer can make recommendations, those "recommendations should reflect to the best of your ability your understanding of clients' circumstances, values and non-legal concerns." The text asserts, "without pretending to be an 'amateur psychologist,' you can build rapport by responding to clients' emotions as well as to the substance of their problems." While these are excellent points, I believe this approach undervalues two critical factors inherent in a lawyer-client relationship. First, one of the reasons the client hired the lawyer was to obtain the benefit of that lawyer's expertise. Of course, it is necessary to respect the client's circumstances and values, but the lawyer also has an obligation to suggest solutions based on the lawyer's experience and expertise as well as on the client's values and desires. Lawyers who limit their role to operating within the client's world view are withholding part of the service they were hired to provide.

Second, while it is important to respond to clients' feelings, so they know they are being heard, it is dangerous for the lawyer to respond so fully that clients take this as an affirmation that their feelings are accurate reflections on reality. In responding sympathetically to a client's emotions, the lawyer must avoid giving advice that may distort the presenting issue or obscure the limits of what the legal system can offer. The reintroduction of the concept of detached legal advice offers a step toward more objective advice for clients and improved emotional health for lawyers.

Beware of Alcohol and Drugs

It is no secret that alcohol is our profession's preferred social lubricant. Liquor is poured at our conferences, bar gatherings, social affairs, and whenever we gather to relax after work. Drinks at lunch have become less common but have not disappeared. For most lawyers, alcohol is not a problem, but for others it is either a potential problem or on its way to becoming a debilitating disease.

Recreational drugs such as marijuana are becoming more accepted and even legal in many places. Some lawyers use other substances regularly. A lawyer can develop a substance abuse problem long before recognizing that the substance has become the problem. By then it may be too late. People with substance abuse addiction usually deny the problem. They will resist help and may continue use to the point where they jeopardize everything they have worked to achieve. National studies reveal devastating facts for lawyers and law students. The studies found that 21–36% of lawyers were "problem drinkers," that 28% had experienced some level of depression, and 11% had experienced suicidal thoughts. This is about twice the rate for the general population. The news was no better for law students. Twenty-five percent of law students were at risk of developing alcoholism, 17% were experiencing depression, 14% were suffering from severe anxiety, and 6% had suicidal thoughts in the past year.[iv] Clearly, our profession has a problem.

Help Lawyers at Risk

Most jurisdictions now have some sort of program designed to identify lawyers at risk of substance abuse before they hurt their clients and ruin their careers. In most communities, other lawyers know where the problems are. Developing a professional culture that encourages reaching out to affected lawyers is a challenge, but it is a far better approach than letting the problem fester until it does real damage to the lawyers, their clients, and the public.

When I was working with the Virginia Lawyers Helping Lawyers program,[v] I was asked to check up on a lawyer in a small town who was reported to be drunk regularly. I did not know the man and was not sure how to approach him. I did have one friend who had moved there several years before and had started her own practice. I called her and said I was just checking to see if any lawyers in the area might benefit from the services of Lawyers Helping Lawyers. I did not mention the man's name because I did not want to put him in a negative light. Without hesitation, my friend blurted out, "Oh, you must mean Fred. Everybody knows Fred's got a real drinking problem." She knew, and so did every other lawyer and judge in town. The problem is real, it is widespread, and it is right under our noses.

No law student or lawyer wants to admit to a drinking or drug problem. All will be fully armed with excuses and justifications for why it is just not a problem for them. Few lawyers can blow the whistle on themselves, and even fewer want to confront another lawyer about drinking or drug use. But if someone suspects there is a problem, pay attention. When other people suggest a person is drinking or using to excess, that is an obvious red flag. Normal drinkers go unnoticed; the lawyer who attracts notice is not normal. Reaching out to that lawyer is an act of compassion toward the lawyer, the family, and our profession.

Avoid Overwork

There is no magic formula for lawyers to maintain their well-being. Books and articles on balancing work and home life are popular. But most lawyers would agree that at any given time, one part of the work/life equation is always going to be out of balance. Either we are stressed and working too much, or we are stressed about finding enough good work. For lawyers, perfect work/life balance is a myth. The best we can do is discipline ourselves to create healthy boundaries between professional work, family duties, and leisure time.

Fear is a common driver for most overworked lawyers: fear that they will make a mistake; fear of an adversary's next move; fear that supervisors or clients will be dissatisfied with their work. With experience, lawyers come to understand that they are always going to make mistakes, are always vulnerable to an adversary, and are always subject to the whims of employers or clients. Nurturing this fear simply adds more unnecessary stress. To offset fear, prepare carefully. If the lawyer is prepared by having digested the facts, researched the law, and developed a strategy, any residual fear is counterfeit. Remember that while you may be awed by the adversary, the adversary has a corresponding feeling about you. The adversary's case is not perfect, and the adversary fears the opposing lawyer will soon discover exactly why. Thus, fear is a two-way street. Regardless of their bravado, bluff, and bluster, adversaries' cases have bad facts they want to keep secret. Keep in mind that the client or your firm chose you to handle the case, rejecting other possible choices. I have never met a senior lawyer who does not remember well how clueless he felt as a new associate. You were chosen because others concluded you could do it.

Some lawyers take a perverse pride in being busy. They seem almost proud to be able to cancel family events or leisure time so they can respond to the next client emergency. Some even seem so eager to jump in, they fail to think through whether it really is an emergency. The thrill of the chase overpowers their need for some respite. Embracing a culture of busyness is dangerous. It imposes long-term stress, which has physical and mental consequences. It decreases creativity and clouds judgment. Rather than striving to be a busy lawyer, aim to become an effective one.

Weigh the Personal Toll

Once I was representing some investors who acquired a national entertainment company. They bought it because although the company was spiraling downward, it had real potential to be turned around and sold at a substantial premium. One of their goals was to reduce costs by cutting wages. My role was to negotiate wage cuts in their labor contracts. Rejecting my advice to take a slower, deliberate approach, the company decided to push ahead for immediate gain.

This move precipitated a long legal fight. In the process, the client fired me, and I ended up being a witness in a long trial. Today, just thinking about this case makes my stomach churn. I had done good legal work and developed a strong strategy, but I got overruled by the client. In the end, the former client prevailed, but I paid a heavy personal price for their victory.

Most lawyers live through a case like this at some point in their career. If a lawyer practices long enough, it is unavoidable. Only years later was I able to embrace the lesson I learned here. Sometimes a lawyer just must refuse a client's instructions. The instructions may be neither unlawful nor unethical. But when the instructions become oppressive to the lawyer, there is an inherent conflict of interest – between the client's desires and the lawyer's well-being. When clients attempt to put me in a similar spot now, I withdraw and recommend other counsel.

A new lawyer working in a law firm may not have that choice. But when this happens, she needs to pass the decision up the line immediately, so the resistance or acquiescence comes from a lawyer in the firm willing to accept responsibility – and take the heat – for the firm's decision.

Another case that has haunted me is the client who was fired from a large healthcare corporation where he worked in internal sales. He thought he was performing well, but his sales territory just kept shrinking. One day when he was on the road visiting customers, his manager and the company HR director showed up and abruptly terminated his employment. He was devastated. A friend referred him to me, and I said I would be happy to talk with him to see if there might be any legal recourse for his discharge and, if there were, I would set him up with the best plaintiff's lawyer I knew.

When he came in for his appointment, he was disheveled, in physical pain, and smelled of cigarette smoke. After listening to his account, I saw several opportunities to make a case of disability discrimination. Since I represented defendants in these cases, I arranged for him to see a leading plaintiff's lawyer. Before that appointment was kept, the friend who referred the salesman called to say he had shot himself and died that morning.

I had not seen this coming. I was shocked. But then I looked back on some troubling signs. In my office, he had been detached, almost withdrawn. He described his situation, including his physical pain, as if it were happening to someone else. He did not seem fully present. He had no enthusiasm for any of the legal alternatives I suggested. When I said I would like to call my friend, the plaintiff's lawyer, he had agreed but showed little interest. Learning of his death, I kept thinking over what I could have done, how I had failed to comprehend the depth of his despair. I had been doing a friend a favor by seeing him. My job was to find him a good referral and I had done that, but I felt I had become collateral damage. This may not have been a reasonable or compassionate reaction, but it was the one I had.

The worst part was my delayed reaction. Suddenly, in my mind, every tale of woe I had ever heard presented itself all over again. The once unconscious strain of bearing client burdens for almost 50 years entered my consciousness and began to crush me. For days, I became resentfully self-absorbed. My duty to keep secrets never expires and I honor that, but this one incident uncovered the pain I had been carrying for decades. In the weeks following, I ruminated on all of this. Had much of my legal career been just a way to buffer clients from the painful consequences of their own decisions and behavior? I have no answer. But in an adversarial system of law based on representing humans, no lawyer emerges unscathed. Professionalism has a cost, and that cost is sometimes paid by the lawyer.

Keep Your Finances in Order

There was a time when lawyers were among the highest-paid members of a community. But now with student loan debt, alternative sources of legal advice, and a larger supply of lawyers to meet demand, the situation has changed. Salary and bonus competition among law firms seeking to attract new graduates cannot obscure the reality that most beginning lawyers have tight budgets. A license to practice law is no longer a guarantee of economic prosperity, but with intelligent planning, a legal career can still offer an economically secure, comfortable living.

No matter what a lawyer earns, if she spends less than she earns, economic security is almost guaranteed. Lawyers' incomes sometimes fluctuate. Bad years follow good ones. The economy tanks or the lawyer's specialty falls out of favor. Even salaried lawyers have taken pay cuts in hard times. Because firms tend to be economically conservative, salaries and bonuses seldom rise as quickly as the economy recovers. But the secret to weathering the lean years is to hold back in the good ones. Beware the infamous golden handcuffs, wherein you are well paid but have a lifestyle that equals your salary. You may feel locked in a firm you would otherwise leave. If your spending is predicated on next year's anticipated income, you will fall short in the long term. If, however, that gap between income and expense is saved and invested, it provides both a more secure future and a financial base to support a career move.

School debt, home mortgages, and car loans may be inescapable. But budgeting to pay them off as soon as possible makes more sense than making minimum payments and incurring interest. For most lawyers, paying down debt does not mean trading affluent living for a hand-to-mouth existence. It means only a moderate belt-tightening to reduce interest fees. The savings create long-term opportunities.

Early on in my first job, I met a financial advisor who suggested I contribute a hundred dollars a month to a fund he was selling. Back then, I did not have a hundred dollars a month in leftover income. We were living paycheck to paycheck and by the end of each month, my credit card was carrying a balance, only to be relieved by my next paycheck. I was fortunate enough to have married a frugal woman who made sure we always had something in our savings account. But that advisor's advice is, nevertheless, still valid. Making it a priority to invest early in a career, even in small amounts, pays enormous dividends 30 or 40 years later. A friend of mine refers to this as the "miracle of compounding." It is a simple principle: small investments can grow into major assets. Money is a tool. Taking a long-term view of money gives the lawyer more control to navigate the future.

Takeaway Tips

Remain balanced
Maintain emotional distance
Beware of alcohol and drugs
Help lawyers at risk
Avoid overwork
Weigh the personal toll
Keep your finances in order.

Notes

i Patrick R. Krill, JD, LLM, Ryan Johnson, MA, and Linda Albert, MSSW, "The Prevalence of Substance Use and Other Mental Health Concerns among American Attorneys," *Journal of Addiction Medicine*, Volume 10, Number 1, January/February 2016.

ii David Binder, Paul Bergman, Paul Tremblay, and Ian Weinstein, *Lawyers as Counselors: A Client-Centered Approach* (4th ed.), Wolters Kluwer, 2019.

iii Id. at 2.

iv "The Prevalence of Substance Use and Other Mental Health Concerns among American Attorneys," *Journal of Addiction Medicine*, Volume 10, Number 1, January/February 2016; "Suffering in Silence: The Survey of Law Student Well-Being and the Reluctance of Law Students to Seek Help for Substance Use and Mental Health Concerns," *Journal of Legal Education*, Volume 66, Number 1, Autumn 2016.

v Now the Virginia Judges and Lawyers Assistance Program, funded primarily by the Virginia State Bar.

CHAPTER XIII

Exploring Other Paths

On September 6, 1995, with the Baltimore Orioles game on TV in the background, one of my law students was at our home, berating me for still using the AOL web browser. I had asked him for help in getting my home office adapted to the web. My student loved tech and was dismayed at my primitive setup. "JB," he said, "you need to get Netscape. AOL is over." When he finished downloading Netscape, we heard a roar from the TV in the next room and watched Cal Ripken, Jr. round the bases to set the baseball record for the most consecutive games ever played.

For me, the significance of that night was not Ripken's record but getting to know my student better. After he graduated from law school, this student took a job with a legal technology company. When he called on our law firm to show how technology could help our practice, my former partners were not impressed. "He's a law graduate," one of them said. "Why does he want to mess with this stuff?" Over the years, my former student persisted and organized his own company. He then sold it to Google, becoming one of their high-ranking executives, and later, taking other jobs, his scope continued to expand.

My partners missed the point. I do not know if my former student has ever written a contract or represented a client, but he is a legal star. He saw an opportunity to bring law and technology together. From that vision, he set out on a career of transforming organizations. And he started by attending law school. In fact, he began disrupting legal education while still in law school by creating the world's first exclusively online law review. Law school was his foundation for an outstanding, transformative career.

Envision Your Future

Not everyone who attends law school intends to practice law. Some know that even before they matriculate. Others figure it out during law school, and still others discover, in the early years of practice, that being a lawyer does not fulfill them. One of the difficulties in describing law graduates who do not intend to practice law or who practice only briefly, is that they do not fall into neat

DOI: 10.4324/9781003533672-14

categories. A few are quite intentional. They go to law school because they believe familiarity with the legal system is an essential component of a career they have in mind – a career outside of law practice. These students often combine other degrees such as an MBA, PhD, or MD with their law degree because these credentials provide a path to their own career goals. These careers may be in law-related service areas such as legal publishing, legal temporary services, expert witness work, or legal consulting. But they may also include other businesses or services that provide entrepreneurial opportunity.

Opinions vary on whether a legal education is good preparation for another career. One prominent lawyer, the managing partner of a national law firm, told me there was no reason for anyone to go to law school who did not intend to practice law. He argued that the many outstanding graduate programs in the United States offered better preparation for a business or consulting career than did law school. Yet others contend that the mode of thinking acquired in law school translates well to a business, consulting, or an entrepreneurial career. Ultimately, the utility of law school will depend on how the individual uses it to advance his own calling. Law school is what you make it – a ticket to the bar exam or the gateway to a different opportunity.

Consider Alternatives

Today, the confluence of three social and economic trends makes legal education relevant to other endeavors. First, the limits that formerly defined law practice have eroded. Territory once clearly within the bounds of law practice has been taken over by products and services not subject to bar regulation. Estate planning and corporate formation documents, including advice on how and when to use them, are sold as software by legal publishers. Land transactions are handled by realtors and title companies, tax work by accountants. Employment consultants advise employers about how to comply with labor and employment laws. While this trend could be seen as diminishing opportunity for law graduates, in fact it represents a growing opportunity for a new generation of legally trained entrepreneurs. Whether these emerging industries encroach on the unauthorized practice of law is a topic largely avoided by state bars. The economic interests supporting the providers are better funded than the bars themselves. The bar has put itself in something of a bind by, on one hand, decrying the gap in providing legal services for the underserved, while on the other hand, resisting creative ways to address those legal issues without hiring a lawyer.

If law graduates wish to participate in the growing legal services industry without having to pass a bar exam or subjecting themselves to the rules of practicing law, the doors are wide open. There has always been a major gap between society's legal needs and the bar's ability to meet them. Creative minds are using technology to close the gap. Technology allows lawyers to become more efficient, just as it allows other providers to offer products as substitutes for traditional legal work. Where unmet legal needs persist, there will be ample opportunity for legally trained entrepreneurs to offer solutions. In a culture where people turn to the internet to solve their romantic and medical problems, it only makes sense for them to seek legal advice in the same place. What it may lack in quality is balanced against ease of access.

A second factor makes legal education relevant to other endeavors: the predictable career path the law once offered has become much less predictable. When I came to the bar, my generation's career expectations were straightforward. A lawyer took a job with a firm, progressed to partnership, and then retired from the same firm. In the early 1970s, it was almost a breach of etiquette for lawyers at an established firm to jump to another firm. Such a move was seen as disloyal to the people who trained and supported them. This all seems quaint today. Now associates commonly switch firms for better pay or more opportunity. Partners are hired away by clients or other firms. Lawyers leave law practice to buy donut franchises, go to seminary, or start businesses. Career paths have been interrupted by a gig economy.

This should not come as a surprise, because most lawyers work gigs. The normal rhythm of private practice consists of a continuing series of short, intense, repeated periods of involvement with a client. A law firm is simply an organization that captures a stream of work and directs it to the lawyers in the firm most likely to handle it efficiently and profitably. No client or matter carries an expectation of permanency. Specialty practices depend on a constant flow of referrals, but the specialty itself may be transformed by legislation or economics or may even disappear altogether. The lawyers then retool or move on to something else.

A third trend was introduced by a series of economic disruptions. For a time in the 1990s, it became more attractive for graduating college students to borrow money for further education than to enter remunerative employment. While this trend has waxed and waned, it has not disappeared. Educators support education. When job markets are tight, it is natural for educators to suggest to students that they need more education. Some college counselors will argue that a college education is not enough. Undergraduates are persuaded they need an advanced degree to set themselves apart. Students know how to be students and, if there is no compelling work opportunity, attending graduate school might seem like a logical choice. Certainly, it is the choice affirmed by those whose livelihood depends on schools.

For some, legal education opens opportunity in the law; for others, it serves as the springboard to other endeavors. But incurring heavy debt to obtain a JD requires finding a job to carry the burden of that debt. Easy borrowing created an influx of students who otherwise might never have considered law school as an option. While some of these students took to law school naturally, others were dispirited to learn that the American legal system is adversarial, and being comfortable dealing with conflict is an essential personal as well as legal skill. Once experiencing these pressures, some new lawyers seek an early exit from law practice. There is a difference between the skills necessary to achieve academic honors and the skills necessary to become an effective lawyer.

Apply Your Legal Skills

One misconception about law school is that it teaches the law student how to be a lawyer. It does not. Law school teaches students how to think like a lawyer, how to analyze like a lawyer, and how to write like a lawyer. Writing and thinking are connected. Formless, abstract thought translates into loose, inexact writing. Legal analysis involves the application of legal principles to particular facts. Lawyers are trained to make distinctions, which is why lawyers sometimes seem so annoying in conversation. Ordinary people do not converse at the same level of precision as most lawyers. Making distinctions is fundamental to legal thought.

Point of view determines what information is pertinent in advocating a cause. Legal training encourages the student to look at all sides of a situation, because advocating an analysis favoring one point of view necessarily requires analyzing the strengths and flaws of the opposite. The best legal reasoning is concise and compelling. The ability to hone thinking and writing skills to a fine point is a powerful tool for any person involved in leadership or persuasion.

At a deeper level, legal training is about problem-solving. Every case a first-year student reads is the tale of an unresolved conflict. Whether it is the story of Mrs. Palsgraf's encounter with the scales at the railway station or Mr. Baxendale's failure to deliver a crankshaft on time, each reported case is an appellate court's second-guessing a lower court's decision about how a dispute should be resolved. The case method used in law schools focuses the student's mind on legal issues and the rules of law that decide those issues. Once a legally trained person applies this mode of thinking to real business problems, another issue emerges. What is the real problem that needs to be solved here? Training in legal analysis focuses the mind on what the real issues are at the heart of any problem. This skill is effective in many fields of endeavor outside the law.

Even if the law student is more oriented toward a career in business, there are good reasons to complete a legal education. Lawyers are trained to be logical, analytical thinkers. They strive to make their points clearly and concisely using precise vocabulary. This training pushes the law graduate to uncover all the information and issues that must be considered before making any decision. This skill set flows directly from reading hundreds of appellate cases and identifying in each one how changing a single fact of the case may alter the legal conclusion.

Law school training also sharpens organizational skills. It requires unrelenting attention to detail. Law students are encouraged to identify the values that underlie the legal rules. Then they can better understand why the legal rules may apply in some situations but not in others. In the broadest sense, law school trains students to think about decisions in a structured way. This may be one of the reasons that most lawyers like to tell stories. Stories are deliberate arrangements of events strung together to make a compelling tale. Writers tell stories for the beauty of the tale itself or for the insight stories afford into human character. Lawyers arrange facts into narratives for a different purpose. Their stories are intended to persuade. Likewise, all lobbyists, businesspeople, consultants, entrepreneurs, and politicians construct stories to present a view of reality that supports the point of view they are advocating.

Risk aversity is inherent in legal training. Thus, the education process itself trains lawyers to avoid mistakes. Now trained to avoid risks, lawyers focus on those aspects of a transaction that present the highest risk. Socratic questioning uncovers how a slight change of circumstance affects the applicability of a legal principle. Legal training spotlights risk and how to avoid it. Some lawyers fall into the trap of seeing risk avoidance as a goal rather than as a tool. Their advice is sometimes directed more at keeping clients safe than encouraging their success. But even risk-avoidant training can have an upside. It tempers the businessperson's higher tolerance for risk with prudent reality, balancing speculation against calculated return. An appreciation of how a deal can fail may restrain unbridled optimism. Thus, legal skills translate well into other areas. Spotting key issues may come naturally to some, but legal training sharpens that ability.

There can be an oddly symbiotic relationship between the urge to become an entrepreneur and the desire for legal training. While a class discussion may concentrate on applicable legal principles, the student with an entrepreneurial bent thinks about what could have been done differently to both avoid the problem and achieve the goal. Lawyers are trained to detest mistakes. Entrepreneurs are more pragmatic. Heading down the wrong path, spotting the mistake, and then quickly changing course is, for them, business as usual. Lawyers are more comfortable drafting safeguards to avoid the pit than exploring ways to capture the peaks. Learning to identify problems benefits entrepreneurs, while their desire to reap disproportionate rewards makes them more comfortable with risk.

Take the Bar Exam

Law graduates who do not intend to practice often ask whether they should take the bar exam. Law school, the bar exam, and law practice are three distinct endeavors. Generally, law school is a three-year, full-time effort. The bar exam is a short, intense sprint to a professional license. In most places, practicing law still requires passing the bar exam.

For those not intending to practice law, there are straightforward reasons why they should not take the bar exam. Passing the exam requires several months of concentrated study and confers a license the graduate may never need. Yet there are obviously advantages to having a bar license. The law is a caste system. Lawyers are members of the club. Jane Smith, Esquire and Jane Smith, JD have completely different connotations. Some law graduates take the bar and then, almost immediately, take inactive status at the bar. This preserves their professional status while relieving them of professional obligations. They can always re-enter the profession as an active lawyer should the course of their careers open in that direction. Taking the bar soon after law school not only keeps options open but eliminates a huge barrier if entering practice becomes a goal at some later date. In a constantly changing economy, keeping this option open presents more opportunity for the law graduate than foreclosing it.

Takeaway Tips

Envision your future
Consider alternatives
Apply your legal skills
Take the bar exam.

Conclusion

As you stand at the threshold of a legal career, you realize the path was not as direct as you expected. Unforeseen challenges, diversions, and obstacles made it difficult. What you thought studying law would be like came to look quite different from when you began to study it. You have suffered from your own failure to understand and then been amazed at how well you understood.

It would be a mistake to think that with law school and the bar exam behind you, the future will bear no resemblance to the past. The process now begins anew, except that you have more control over where the path leads and how you want to shape your career.

Our culture depends on the rule of law. It depends on lawyers willing to devote themselves to the rule of law. If that sounds somewhat overblown, it is, but it is also true. Our system is flawed, often corrupt and systemically oppressive, but it is a system that can recognize its faults and begin to correct them, albeit not perfectly. Years from now, the system, still imperfect, will look different, and the difference will be shaped by the decisions made by today's new lawyers. Your decision on how to spend your career will play its part in making that difference.

Shortly after leaving law school and taking the bar exam, I was privileged to spend some time with Stanislas Aquarone, then Registrar of the International Court of Justice. Mr. Aquarone, a sprightly, spirited man, was explaining to me his role with the Court and one of the cases they had recently decided. Although I listened intently, I responded as only an arrogant, self-assured, recently graduated law student could. "But, Mr. Aquarone, no one pays any attention to those decisions of the World Court." He replied swiftly and precisely. "No, JB, some don't." He became silent for about ten seconds then added, "But in 300 years they will." He was taking the long view. He was perfectly aware of the Court's current limitations. But he also understood that the processes and reach of the rule of law evolve over time. The law now will not be the law forever. But what we do now, insignificant as it may seem at present, moves the cause of justice forward. We may never have the satisfaction of knowing how our work makes any difference. We can assure ourselves, however, that our work becomes part of the great force of history that presses forward resolutely to create a more just world.

DOI: 10.4324/9781003533672-15

Just as law school was a challenging transition from college, so law practice is a dramatic transition from law school. Most lawyers say it takes about five years after passing the bar to become comfortable as a practicing lawyer. This is a craft as well as an art, and a craft requires repetition and adjustment before the basic techniques are mastered. An art requires the application of intuition to the combination of intelligence and experience.

Not long ago, toward the end of a contentious meeting, I had finally convinced a client to see a problem in terms that client had previously resisted. After the meeting ended and the client had left, my associate turned to me and asked, "How did you do that?" My answer was that I didn't know. After practicing law for a long time, I had developed some skills. I had learned when to listen and when to keep silent. I spoke when the client was ready to listen. Maybe it was the silence; maybe it was the timing. I really don't know.

My legal career has had its disappointments. I remember staying up all night to finish a memo the partner never read. I remember getting no more than a day-and-a half off for the birth of each of our two sons. I have cut vacations short or cancelled them altogether. I have represented clients whose greed kept other people from getting money they needed. I have travelled when I should have stayed home sick. I have missed milestones in the lives of my family. But I'm not complaining. When you accept the obligations of a license to practice law, your schedule is not entirely within your control. While I have more happy and satisfied memories than painful ones, honesty requires disclosing both. There is a price to carrying other people's burdens. Not understanding this at the outset leads to disillusion and bitterness. This is not a profession for the lazy or faint-of-heart.

Despite this, I love being a lawyer. I have never wanted to do anything else. It is a privilege to help extricate clients from desperate situations. There is joy in finding a solution to a Gordian knot of a problem. There is honor in being trusted and relied upon. There is dignity in being able to speak for those who cannot speak for themselves and to advance a cause just because it is right. There is satisfaction, even in the depths of contention and controversy, in embracing your role as a peacemaker.

In whatever way you participate in the legal profession, you will make your mark. When successful lawyers practice law, all their professional skills are filtered through their unique selves. Your dreams cannot come true if you are playing a role, not being yourself. Centering your practice on who you are provides the advantage of never sounding a false note. Your own voice carries its own credibility. It is authentic.

So, now it is up to you. You have come this far. You are ready. You have everything you need to make the difference only you can make. There is nothing to fear. Go for it.

INDEX

For Product Safety Concerns and Information please contact our EU
representative GPSR@taylorandfrancis.com
Taylor & Francis Verlag GmbH, Kaufingerstraße 24, 80331 München, Germany

www.ingramcontent.com/pod-product-compliance
Ingram Content Group UK Ltd.
Pitfield, Milton Keynes, MK11 3LW, UK
UKHW020000200926
475702UK00015B/2390
9781032876290